How To Have A Business Not A Job

WITHOUT NEARLY KILLING YOURSELF

Mark Creedon

MELBOURNE, AUSTRALIA

Mark Creedon c/- Intertype
Unit 45, 125 Highbury Road
BURWOOD VIC 3125
www.intertype.com.au

Book Layout ©2020 Intertype Self-Publishing Services

Ordering Information:
Quantity sales. Special discounts are available on quantity purchases by corporations, associations and others. For details, contact the "Special Sales Department" at the address above.

How to Have a Business Not a Job / Mark Creedon. —1st ed.
ISBN 978-0-6488639-0-8

Contents

"If you can keep your head while all about you are losing theirs and blaming it on you"

- Rudyard Kipling

Acknowledgment

This book is just a small glimpse of my experience as a professional Business Coach. It is as much from the wisdom and experience of my amazing clients as it is from me. It would therefore be wrong if I did not acknowledge the insight and wisdom I have gained from the brave entrepreneurs I have worked with over the past fifteen years.

As with any labour of love, as this book certainly was, there are so many more people behind the scenes than just the author. I want to dedicate this book to those who have helped me on my entrepreneurial journey, not just in the completion of this book.

Thanks to Jack Harding who coached me to the next level and helped remove some of the roadblocks that were holding me back as a coach and a businessowner. I also want to thank my business partner, mentor and star coaching client Michael Yardney for his wisdom, support, encouragement and most of all, for his friendship.

None of what I do would be worth doing if it wasn't for my family. My father Mike serves as a constant source of wisdom and inspiration even 26 years after his death. My Mother, Merle who I miss everyday taught me to not take no for an answer and to chase my dreams. To my son Nicholas, daughter Samantha, son in law Leroi and daughter in law De and my gorgeous grandchildren, Iziah, Archer and Elouise, thank you for your unconditional love and support. Thank you also to Samantha for being my long suffering editor and publishing liaison. This book would never have happened without you.

Finally, everything we do in business and in life is made so much easier, more enjoyable and rewarding with the love and support of a life partner. In Caroline I have all that and an awesome business partner as well. Thanks babe!

Introduction

As a child I was taught that success only came from either extraordinary good luck or extremely hard work. My parents worked hard. Mum, for many years, held the traditional role of stay at home mother and housekeeper whilst dad went to work. They were both extraordinary people and taught me so much of the wisdom I carry with me today, but they also taught me some things I had to spend decades unlearning.

They believed that being rich was a dirty word and that the truly wealthy people were either born into it, won it or engaged in some unsavoury illegal business to gain it. So, the thought of being truly wealthy was always a terrible struggle for me. From a young age I decided that I didn't want to buy in to my parents' theory of wealth creation but I also felt guilty for having those opposing thoughts. I grew up in a working class suburb and I am very proud of that. I had a great childhood with great friends. All of my friend's parents were working class people who worked hard, earned a basic wage and lived a modest lifestyle. Holidays were mostly taken at home, staycations rather than vacations and luxuries consisted of monthly take aways. I knew in my heart that I was destined for more than that. What I didn't know was how and ultimately, I chose a "how" which would cost me the very success I craved.

You see, as I grew up and I shared my desire with friends and their parents I would often be met with retorts like "oh so you are too good for us, are you?" Or 'well I suppose once you have made lots of money you won't be coming around here anymore'. My thoughts were actually far from that. I was proud of my upbringing and I thought that those friendships could last a lifetime. Even then I thought that if I could be more successful than my friends that I would be able to show them how and "bring them along for the journey with me".

As time progressed and my parents realised that I wasn't going to leave school and just get a job like my three older brothers, I think they found themselves conflicted. I know they loved me and wanted to support me but their love for me also meant that they didn't want me to be disappointed.

Many years later I now encourage my grandsons to aim for the stars and its okay if they slightly miss. When she is old enough, I will encourage my granddaughter in the same way. My parents however would encourage me to lower the sights in case I missed and was disappointed. That difference in thinking has taken me decades of learning, many thousands of dollars in courses and mentoring as well as countless days of heartache for me and those closest to me as they watched me self-destruct.

So, the only way I could resolve the conflict was to reject only part of my parent's beliefs on success and accept some of them. The part I chose to accept was that the only way you could achieve success was to work hard and the only way you could gain and then maintain wealth was to work even harder. I have always had a strong work ethic and I have my parents to thank for that. They taught me the meaning of a hard day's work and the value of the money earned from it. But they also left me believing that I had to work my arse off for 45 years, retire at 65 with a modest nest egg and then start to enjoy life until I died. What a shit philosophy (sorry Mum, my mother never swore but in moments of utter frustration she would spell it s.h.i.t, somehow that's not as bad as actually saying it! She would crack me up and I miss her every day).

That's what I did. When I was 17 I started studying nursing.

At 19 I went to university to study business and law. I had a fulltime job, went to university three nights a week and worked two nights a week polishing floors at Kmart. I bought my own home when I was 20 and my second property when I was 25. At 26 I had my own business working with clients all over Australia and I was at every level achieving the success I envisaged. At 27 my daughter Samantha was born, at 30 my son Nicholas came along and things could not have been better. By

34 I was separated from my childhood sweetheart, lost most of my possessions and by 36 I was flat broke. I had worked so hard that I barely saw my children and had neglected what I now know really mattered. I had followed the only success formula I knew, work ridiculous hours, focus entirely on work and making money, nothing else mattered. It took me another ten years of floating trying to work out what the hell went wrong.

I had worked so hard I had lost my marriage, I had lost my friends and then my striving for success became so all powerful that it blinded me to the pitfalls, the ones I fell right into and tumbled downwards to rock bottom. Secretly I think my brothers were delighted. I mean, who did I think I was anyway to dare to think that I could climb out of my birthright to be working class. If that wasn't low enough I woke up one morning after a night of abject misery, drowning in the fact that I had tried, succeeded and then failed spectacularly that I had drunk a bottle of whiskey, which is why I passed out. The only reason I woke is because my partner at the time, Julie was waking me, crying, screaming at me. I stirred slowly and tried to focus and then I saw what was causing her so much upset. There, hanging from the rafter on our back deck was the noose I had tied and the stool I had placed to take my own life…..with my true purpose and destiny still inside me. Thank god for whiskey which caused me to pass out or I would never have gotten to write these words today.

That is what ultimately brought me to coaching. The only 'secret' to success which I had known had in fact been very unsuccessful. I had no idea how to do things differently and I was too proud to ask for help (another thing my parents taught me which can be a double-edged sword.) I knew that I had a natural ability to get quickly to the real motivation behind their actions. I also knew I had a natural ability to help others to see how they could be their best. It was with that knowledge that I decided to study Psychology and ultimately use that qualification and my business experience (oh and a few lessons from the school of life) to start coaching.

The purpose of this book is to help you to have a business and learn the lessons I did, just in a much easier way. I want to show you how hard work may be necessary to get you to success; but how continued success doesn't have to depend on your continued hard work. I want to show you how to get the balance between business and "life" that I missed. I also want to show you how the real secret to success in business comes from learning, asking questions, seeking advice and relying on others. In business it can be lonely enough without doing what I did and believing you have to be an island.

Finally, I want you to see that setting goals and targets is actually quite simple and if you follow a process then achieving them is too. You don't have to lower your aim in case you don't get there and you certainly don't have to subconsciously destroy it all just because deep down you've been conditioned to believe that you shouldn't be aiming for it and therefore don't deserve it.

This book, much like the Mastermind program I have written, is designed to work on you so that you can in turn work on your business. Whilst playing the role of Patch Adams, Robin Williams once said " if you treat the disease, you win or you lose, but if you treat the person you win every single time"

Thank you for taking the time to treat yourself with this book, it is designed to treat you!

How To Get The Best From This Book

This book is designed to coach you. It has been written by a coach and is a combination of thousands of hours of coaching business owners. It is not a reference book but more like an extended coaching session or a workshop. The book contains exercises, for you to complete as you go, worksheets to make those exercises as simple as possible and a whole heap of resources to help you to grow a million dollar business without killing yourself, getting divorced or your kids hating you because you are never there. Once set up, a business should be able to largely run itself with the help of the people who you have empowered to maintain it so that you can be the person you want to be, to the people who matter most to you.

CHAPTER 1

Let's Build Your Level 3 Business Without Nearly Killing Yourself In The Process

One of the secrets to growing a successful business is to make sure that you are making the highest and best use of the time you commit to it. When we start in business, we often have to do everything ourselves, we are the receptionist, the tea and coffee maker, business development manager, sales manager and CEO of a small business. It's what I call a level 1 business which simply means you do it all and have neither control nor freedom (and very likely you don't have much money either!).

After a while you grind your way to the next level. You have brought on some people in some capacity to help you and you are starting to gain a little control of the business. You have plans that are starting to come to fruition, revenue is starting to steady out. The problem is that the business still relies heavily on you. You now have a level two business. You have control but no freedom.

What I want to do is to help you get to level three, where the business operates largely without you, systems and processes are in place and you actually have time to work "on " the business rather than "in" it. Now you have both control and freedom and at this level you also have a steady and lucrative income.

Getting to level three takes commitment and time, but the important thing about time is to make sure you are spending it doing the right things. We have all seen various time management programs, matrixes and the like. Sure, they are all really valuable but the biggest issue I had when growing my business was that they were way too complicated. I needed to list my tasks, allocate them a grading or a code, list them on a grid, transfer that to a worksheet. It all became too complicated and I felt like I spent as much time planning as I did doing. I fell into that awful trap of thinking it was just easier to go head down and bum up and get shit done. This alone led me to start looking for a simpler and more effective way.

Let's look at some simple ways that you can get more time to spend doing the right things in your business.

CHAPTER 2

Scale your Time

"Time is free, but it's priceless.

You can't own it, but you can use it.

You can't keep it, but you can spend it.

Once you've lost it you can never get it back."

Harvey Mackay

In order to get to level three you need to learn how to scale your time

First of all, we need to understand what 'time' we are speaking of. Most people in small business or in a professional practice will think of time as a commodity which generates revenue directly. In other words, they talk about trading time for money. This is exactly the mouse wheel that I want to help you get off.

A few years ago I got a phone call from a client called John, the start of the conversation went like this, "Mark, I need to change my name". Conversations which start like this are bound to pique one's interest and it certainly did mine. When we dug down a little bit deeper I discovered that the reason he wanted to change his name was because he was tired of everybody in his business constantly using it. In other words he became the go to person. A colleague of mine often and says that when he first walked in to a business as a coach the first thing he asked is who do I speak to if the photocopier is broken and if it's a business owner then he knows there is some serious work to do in that business. John fell fairly and squarely into that category. He was the go to person. Anything that needed to be done in his business everyone in the business called his name. John was completely trapped, not only was he the go to person for his clients now it had become an internal problem as well.

Now you maybe in a small service business a very small professional practice and you may right now be thinking that's the only way I can operate, I have to be the go-to person. In that case, you actually don't have a business. What you have is a job.

This is how we solved John's problem. We realised that being a service professional, there are two invaluable truths about his business. Firstly clients expect to see him. Secondly he is the only one in his business with the qualifications and expertise to deliver. What we needed to do therefore was to find a way in which we could either free up some of John's time or alternatively make sure that the time he was spending was spent in the most effective and efficient purposes.

I believe that cashflow follows your calendar. That simply means that what you do, where you spend your time will dictate the revenue your business generates. It works in that order though and generally not in reverse. You need to focus effort and planning into where you spend your time and on which tasks in order to have greater control.

To get on top of time, there are two simple techniques. First we:

- Understand negative time and then
- Allocate priorities correctly

Let's look at negative time first. There are four types of negative time:

1. Unplanned time

2. Interrupted time

3. Wasted time

4. Low Value time

Working through these one by one and making sure you have each of these negative time influencers under control will give you significant control and freedom. It will enable you to truly scale the time you have so that you can focus it on the right priorities. We will get to the priorities management once we have these time demons under control.

---

1. UNPLANNED TIME:

Have you ever wondered how it is that successful people get so much done in their day? I mean let's be honest we all only have 24 hours in the day. It can be easy to put it down to the fact that they have lots of people to delegate things to (and we will come to that when we look at low value time) but the reality is that they understand the benefit of planning and their planning starts first thing in the morning.

If you want to get the jump start on the day and achieve more than you ever have then there are three simple steps to follow:

1. Have a morning routine

2. Block out time in your calendar to work on your business

3. Remove distractions so you can stay focused.

I have a simple morning routine. I get up at around 5 or 5.30am. I spend thirty minutes reading something insightful. It may be a business book, an article or blog, something which is going to further my knowledge and inspire me to take action. Something which improves me.

After I have read I spend about 20 minutes writing in my journal. This helps me to focus on the priorities, not for the day but for my life. I take the time to journal about the life lessons I have learned the day before and the positives I can take from them. I also take some time toward the end of my journal entry to acknowledge what I have to be grateful for. Sometimes it's a significant win in my business or a major win I know a client has had. Sometimes it is just being grateful for the fact that I get to sit on my balcony overlooking the ocean each morning. What this journaling does though is to place things in the right order for me. I think about what I have learned and therefore what I can take forward with me, what I need to leave behind and then the final gratitude exercise sets the positive mind set for the rest of the day. It's a bit like it doesn't matter what the world might throw at me today, I have things to be very grateful for.

Once I have finished journaling I go through my email inbox and answer the pressing emails, send the ones I want to get started on early so that others can be working on them throughout the day and either delegate, delay or delete the rest. Going through that process gives me clarity to the day, clears the backlog of emails and sets expectations for me and others before the day is too far underway. Once I have the emails dealt with, I then write out my daily to do lists, the projects I want to get completed that day. I already have my regular daily, weekly and monthly tasks in my calendar (I will show you how to do that shortly) so all I need to allocate time for is the tasks which have come up in the last 24 hours or which may have come from dealing with my emails that morning.

So, what is your morning routine? If you don't have one, make a start right now. Grab a pen and paper and think about what a productive morning routine looks like for you and before you say that its not possible because you are not a morning person I have to tell you that neither am I. On the weekends I love a sleep in and will think nothing of lying in bed until 9am or later!

My Morning Routine Planner

Get up at: _____

___ Minutes read to learn

___ Minutes emails

___ Minutes planning

___ Minutes moving/exercise

"If you win the morning, you win the day"

-Tim Ferris

What I did was train myself on a new routine and simply practice it until it became a habit and you can do the same. Please don't rule this out because you don't think you can get up at 5 am. That's fine it is far more about the actual routine than the hour of the day. There is a saying that if you win the morning you win the day, so claim your morning whatever time that may start for you. Remember it is about how you plan your day, the order of things. This wonderful fable, told many times over and in many different ways by a number of authors is a timely (no pun intended) reminder.

A professor stood before his philosophy class and had some items in front of him. When the class began, he wordlessly picked up a very large and empty mayonnaise jar and proceeded to fill it with golf balls. He then asked the students if the jar was full. They agreed that it was.

The professor then picked up a box of pebbles and poured them into the jar. He shook the jar lightly. The pebbles rolled into the open areas between the golf balls. He then asked the students again if the jar was full. They agreed it was.

The professor next picked up a box of sand and poured it into the jar. Of course, the sand filled up everything else. He asked once more if the jar was full. The students responded with an unanimous "yes."

The professor then produced two cups of coffee from under the table and poured the entire contents into the jar, effectively filling the empty space between the sand. The students laughed.

"Now," said the professor as the laughter subsided, "I want you to recognise that this jar represents your life. The golf balls are the important things — your family, your children, your health, your friends and your favourite passions — and if everything else was lost and only they remained, your life would still be full. The pebbles are the other things that matter like your job, your house and your car. The sand is everything else — the small stuff.

"If you put the sand into the jar first," he continued, "there is no room for the pebbles or the golf balls. The same goes for life. If you spend all your time and energy on the small stuff you will never have room for the things that are important to you.

"Pay attention to the things that are critical to your happiness. Play with your children. Take time to get medical check-ups. Take your spouse out to dinner. Play another 18. There will always be time to clean the house and fix the disposal. Take care of the golf balls first — the things that really matter. Set your priorities. The rest is just sand."

One of the students raised her hand and inquired what the coffee represented.

The professor smiled. "I'm glad you asked. It just goes to show you that no matter how full your life may seem, there's always room for a couple of cups of coffee with a friend."

If you want some simple tools to apply this in your business try using our Rock Pebble Sand worksheets to help you allocate the right priorities in your business.

---

2. WASTED TIME

I won't waste a lot of time on this. Imagine if I told you I could help you gain an extra day a week! I imagine you would be pretty impressed however the reality is far less impressive and not at all magical.

There is a difference between wasted time and time which feeds you. If you want to scale your time so that you can move your business to the next level you have to learn how to distinguish between the two. If you really want more time to spend working on your business but feel like there just isn't enough hours in the day, stop and take an honest and critical look at what you do spend your time on.

Spend a week keeping track of the amount of time you watch TV, spend time on social media or reading emails which are never going to help you advance your personal skills nor your business. If we are completely honest with ourselves there will be plenty of time to tap into, it is just a question of priorities and discipline.

Let's say you spend 30 minutes a day watching the news 20 minutes a day reading through Facebook posts from old school friends (just so you can feel better that you don't look as old as they do!) and 10 minutes a day reading emails from some list you subscribed to years ago but are really no longer relevant. That's an hour a day. Even if all we did was take that away on a Monday to Friday you have just gained an extra five hours that week.

You see, it's not that there isn't enough hours in the day, there just isn't enough value placed on the hours you do have. Change the way you value your time and watch the amount of time you gain. Take that gained time and spend it wisely on your business and you are well on your way to a level three operation. I want to be clear about one thing though. I am not advocating that you abandon all fun and joy to work on your business. That would be the very antithesis of the intention of this book. Becoming a slave to your business is like being at level one for eternity, you may as well just have a job!

THE PEBBLE PROCESS

Now it's time to plan your pebbles. First, decide the ideal frequency, duration, and location of your holidays.

Next, list everything you need to do to deliver on your business promise with your clients, and how often each deliverable occurs.

HOLIDAYS

Frequency		
Duration		
Destinations		

DELIVERABLES - Promise to Clients/Customers

Frequency	Frequency	Frequency
Frequency	Frequency	Frequency

BUSINESS
MASTERMIND

THE READY ROCK PLANNER™

	END OF THIS YEAR		END OF NEXT YEAR	
Monthly Revenue				
# of Clients/Customers				
# of Free Days				

MY MONEY MAKING What are the regular things I need to do to make money?	FREQUENCY Monthly, Weekly, Daily

THE SAND SIFTER™

Professional Learning & Development	Personal Family Events	Friends
Planning Days	Birthdays	Hobbies
Team Training	Personal Care - looking after you	Other

BUSINESS
SUCCESS @ MASTERMIND

3. LOW VALUE TIME

In order to scale your time, we have seen from the discussion on wasted time, that you first need to value your time. Once you value your time, you will stop wasting so much of it. The other interesting transformation which will happen is that you will start to assess the value of the tasks you spend your time on.

In a level one business you have to do everything yourself and so it doesn't really matter how much you value your time. The reality is you don't have anyone else in the business to do what must be done. That's why you do it. Similarly, however that's why you don't want your business to remain at level one. This is a common trap that many professional practitioners fall into. They go into a professional practice thinking that doing so will give them higher levels of freedom, control and reward than if they had simply got a job. The problem is that before long the control becomes ingrained and they start to value control over freedom. The irony is that this approach gives you neither. In order to get that control back you have to Learn what is the highest and best use of your time.

Low value tasks are those tasks which can be easily outsourced or delegated and which on an objective assessment will cost you less to delegate or outsource in the value of your time.

For example if you can earn $100 an hour in your business then any task within your business which can be outsourced for delegated for 25 or $30 an hour should be done so immediately. Often the logic of this is irrefutable but it is just taking that leap of faith to let go that is the barrier. When my business was at level one stage my wife who later became my business partner used to do all of our bookkeeping And even though we knew that paying a bookkeeper $90 an hour would free her up to earn revenue at a much higher rate than that there was this great trepidation about letting go of managing the accounts for the business. I have seen this time and time again in level one businesses and professional practices where the business owner simply can't bring themselves to let go thinking that letting go of control exposes them to a whole range of unnecessary risk. This is where you must understand the difference between control and controls. What you want to have in your business is a series of controls so that when you let go of things such as accounts there are structures systems and processes in place to bring any issues to your attention. Having controls, checks and balances in areas such as your accounting will mean that you can immediately mitigate the risk of being ripped off by some unscrupulous person.

Let go of control and replace that with systemised and structured control.

"You don't need to control, merely to have controls."

4. INTERRUPTED TIME

There are three major interrupters to our time.

1. Phone
2. Email
3. People

I read an article recently which suggested that the average adult business owner checks their smart phone some 85 times per day. If we imagined for a moment that each time we checked the phone it took only 30 seconds and that's probably being very generous, then that is 42 ½ minutes each day. If instead we checked the phone 10 times per day and we took three times as long each time that would be 15 minutes in total which means we've saved 27.5 minutes per day. Across a week that's 3.2 hours. Imagine waking up one morning and instantly getting 3.2 hours back in your day. Well congratulations, you can, tomorrow morning! These figures are startling when we consider that the whole idea of smart phones was to make life easier and more productive not less so. It's interesting that smart phone manufacturers now provide the amount of screen time each week just to give us some insight into where we spend our time.

So, the big question is how do we get on top of the phone as an interrupter. Well, the same applies to emails. One of our

Mastermind members was concerned that there just wasn't enough time in the day to work on his business. He was stuck and unable to scale his time. We did a quick assessment of the number of times he checked and dealt with emails. What we discovered was that he was checking his emails an astounding 50 times.

That figure may not seem too astounding at first glance however, when you consider the fact that the checking of the emails on average took about two minutes then that amounted to in excess of 1.5 hours per day just checking emails. Let's add another two minutes in lost time leaving one task to check the email before getting back to that task and we could very easily suggest that there was up to three hours a day of interrupted time. That's 15 hours in a working week or the equivalent of almost two working days!

Let's look at phone calls. Imagine if you batched your phone calls. Try setting dedicated time in your calendar for daily checking of emails and set times for phone calls. You can have separate times for incoming calls and another time for returning calls.

The great thing about mobile phones is that you can turn them off or put them on 'aeroplane' or 'do not disturb' mode. Try it. It may seem a bit scary at first, but you will probably be surprised or perhaps even amazed at how much you get done without the constant interruption of a phone call. If the land line phone is the bain of your life, put it on 'do not disturb' or just take it off the hook.

There are two important 'tricks' here. The first is to be disciplined. You may think it will be easy to set new habits for your phone but once you start you will see just how difficult it is. You have probably developed habits over years not months so it may not be as easy as you think. So, you need to set yourself up a structure that will help with the discipline. Put in your calendar the times you have allocated for your phone. Turn it off at other times and give someone else permission to remind you if you are breaking your new habit. Discipline comes from repetitive practice and commitment to an outcome. Be really clear on the end game here. Imagine your new life of freedom and what you will do with that newfound time that your phone is currently stealing from you.

The second trick is to set expectations. We live in a fast world where the general expectation is for an immediate response. I remember a time when you had to post a letter, wait a week for it to get there, a few days for them to write a response and then a week back in the post. Times have certainly changed but that doesn't always mean for the better.

People expect an immediate response because that is probably what they have always got from you. They call and you dutifully answer. Now you need to set the expectation that you may not and that it may take a period of time for you to respond. Try setting the expectation that you'll return calls in 24 hours initially and see how that works for you. Set your voice message to let people calling you know that you only check your messages twice a day and you'll get back to them within that 24 hour timeframe.

Set messages that set the expectations and it will be hard for people to be disappointed or complain. If that works, try stretching things out a little further. You'll find a rhythm that suits you and once you do, you'll never look back.

Very similar 'tricks' apply to emails. I suggest starting by setting times in your calendar to check your emails. Start at three times a day, morning noon and afternoon. Turn the notifications off. It's okay, even though you don't get the notification the email will still be there. You don't have to be on call 24 hours a day, unless of course you actually do!

If your business is time critical then check your emails at the top of the hour but get into the habit of only dealing with the truly critical matters and leaving the others to dedicated 'other emails' times set in your calendar. Like your phone, set a structure around your new habit and you will be much less likely to fall off the wagon. Ask someone to keep you accountable.

The same as phones, you can also manage the expectations of others using auto responders. Set a response that lets people know you only check your emails at certain times or on certain days and that you will respond within a set time frame. Start with 24 hours and see how that feels. If it really freaks you out that's fine, add something in there that says that if the matter is super urgent you'll deal with it sooner.

I once emailed Naomi Simpson, CEO of Red Balloon and received an email back to say she only checks her emails on Fridays. How cool is that. Now that is really being in control of your inbox. Remember, your inbox is just someone else's priority list. It's time to focus on yours instead.

Now you have time sorted, let's plan to use its better.

CHAPTER 3

Plan For Success

There is an old saying that a failure to plan is a plan to fail. It's one of those sayings I like to describe as "TBU" (true but useless). Why do I think failing to plan is a plan to fail is useless I hear you ask?

Well it's not that it's a useless saying per se. It's more that it's lacking in any real substance. I'm a fan of keeping things simple but this is too far. That saying suggests that any plan is better than none but the reality is that any plan, no matter how simple or how detailed is only as good as its implementation. I couldn't tell you how many times I've consulted with a business for the first time to be told by the CEO or the Board that yes they have a plan and no they haven't worked from it, updated it or even thought about it for a long time.

I've seen business plans in large binders consisting of hundreds of pages pulled from shelves to have the dust blown from them. What's the point? In our Mastermind program we work off a very simple four step approach to planning which enables our business owners to have a crystal clear picture of the four main factors any plan should address:

1. Why
2. What
3. How
4. Now

I am sure many of you will have read Simon Sinek's 'Start with Why' and if you haven't then I encourage you to do so, not yet though. You need to finish reading this book first and then grab a copy, it will reinforce what I am about to help you learn.

Understanding your why will be a fundamental aspect of planning for and successfully running your business. If you are reading this and about to start a business, then take the time set out in this chapter and conduct the exercises to discover your 'why'. If you have been running your business for a while, take the time to reflect and write down your current 'why', its probably different from the one you had when you first started and after reading this book it may very well be different again.

Knowing your "why"

As Stephen Covey said in The 7 Habits of Highly Effective People:

"How different our lives are when we really know what is deeply important to us and keeping that picture in mind, we manage ourselves each day to be and do what really matters most. If the ladder is not leaning against the right wall, every step we take just gets us to the wrong place faster"

When I am presenting these concepts from the stage, I usually start by asking a very simple question. " What do you want more of?" So, what DO you want more of? Some people in business want more money, more time or perhaps more freedom, (of course these just happen to be the very things that we deliver to our Mastermind members but I will tell you more about that later in this book. In the meantime, why not grab a piece of paper and a pen and take a few minutes to think about what it is you want more of.

Okay, done? Well the next step I take with the audience is to pick someone who has a clear picture of what they want and ask them another simple (but a bit dastardly) question, "what will that get you? And so, I repeat that question. To each answer they give I ask again, "What will that get you?" And I keep asking that question until I have an answer which truly resonates with them, one which comes from an emotional truth. So, an initial answer of "I want more money' may become "more time" and eventually " I want to spend more dedicated time with my children playing while they are young" or " "I want to travel with my life partner while we are both still young enough to enjoy the pleasure of travel and experiences". The answers sometime take a while to come but if I keep asking then I know I will breakthrough to that emotional answer eventually. This their true "why". Its why they stay in business, it's probably why they started their own business in the first place and its why they battle through cashflow issues, staffing, legislation changes, taxation debts and all of the other wonderful pleasures which we, as business owners get to experience.

So, take a moment now and ask yourself what will your answer to the question of what you want more of actually get you? You have to be brutal and also brutally honest. If you can't get to the bottom of it for yourself and after a few minutes you are still staring at the page in front of you, get someone to ask you. Pick a friend, a colleague but make sure it's someone who will push you hard for the true answer. It's one of the benefits of being a part of a like-minded group like our Mastermind. In that group if I don't get to ask you that question and push you hard there are plenty of members who are committed to helping you to be your best and they will be only too happy to push you hard!

Take some time now and see what comes from the exercise. The final answer will be the one which resonates with you the most. As Tim Ferris says in The Four Hour Week, answer the question of what excites you. You have to know this before you go any further. Planning your business without getting this right will either lead you to a business which is really no more than a job (and potentially a job you hate) or you won't have the motivation needed to get you through the hurdles which will come. And if you think you may be immune to those hurdles you're not. Almost every business follows a pretty simple growth pattern.

Once you have been able to answer the "why" question then the real planning can begin. In our Mastermind we use a very simple one page planning tool. I use it my business and I have also used with every business I have coached in recent years. In fact, I have used the same tool with simple start-up businesses with no cash flow and little more than a concept all the way through to a business which turns over A$30 million and has a staff of nearly 300.

What do I want more of?

What will that get me?

And what will THAT get me?

And what will THAT get me?

So, what do I REALLY want more of?

I can't claim the credit for this plan. I learned it from Taki Moore from Million Dollar Coach and have used it ever since. Thanks Taki!

Here it is…

YOUR MASTERMIND ONE PAGE BUSINESS PLAN

Use this worksheet to map out your VISION, GOALS, PROJECTS, and ACTIONS.
Review it each Monday and add a new set of weekly actions with a Post-It Note.

30,000' | 3 YEARS | VISION	20,000' | 12 MONTHS | GOALS
10,000' | 90 DAYS | PROJECTS	**RUNWAY | THIS WEEK | ACTIONS**

BUSINESS
MASTERMIND

*Credit to Taki Moore

Of course, if you are looking to raise funds, bring in an investor or list your company on the stock exchange then this plan will absolutely not be enough to meet the requirements. But, simply put and when used with the other simple tools I am going to show you shortly, it's a very cool tool which will more than suffice in the vast majority of cases. Plus, there is a fair chance it is better than the business plan you are working from right now.

Focus on 'WHAT'

Let's have a look at the blank plan and how it works. Starting at the top left hand quarter. This is where you look at your three year goals. What you write here is really more about the "why" we have just discussed. It holds the big picture, why you do what you do. Three years is a long way out especially with how fast the world is moving. Technology in three years will be so far advanced that the landscape of your business may have changed dramatically. This is why I like to focus this part of the plan on your "why". It will help you to stay focused and continue to strive toward that big picture as you complete the rest of the plan and also as you adjust and update it, but more about that a little later.

Let's continue to work our way through the One Page Plan. Before we go much further though let me explain what the numbers on the plan mean. My brother in law, Val is an airline pilot. I am always teasing him about the fact that he works limited hours and sits down for a living. I'm just playing of course. I know his job is actually very stressful and if anything ever went wrong on a flight I would be very comfortable knowing he was at the controls. Anyway, I was talking with Val and he was telling me how a pilot changes their thinking and planning based on the altitude they are flying at. It got me thinking how similar business planning is. So apparently at 30

000 feet pilots are really looking at the big picture, the overall flight plan and just making sure they are staying on track. As they descend into a landing the activity level increases.

At 20,000 feet they start to think about the flightpath into the airport, which runway. In other words, they are then focusing on the goal of getting the aircraft safely on the ground. As they descend further to 10,000 feet, they start taking very specific steps, wheels down flaps adjusted, seatbelt on etcetera. When they hit the runway then that's when the activity level spikes. They are doing much more now, keeping the plane in a straight line, applying brakes and ensuring that it comes to a safe stop at the right gate. This is when there is a lot of activity in the cockpit.

So, it was with that process in mind that I added the figures into the plan. When you are working in the top left quarter you are at the 30,000 feet mark. Your focus is on the big picture. Next you can move across to the top right. These are your more specific goals. In this quarter write out what you want to achieve in twelve months' time. A simple process I use when coaching is to ask, "If we were having a conversation in twelve months and I asked you to tell me about your business, what we would be talking about, what would it look like for you? Take some time and be as clear as you can. To have a bigger business or to have more money is not a goal, that's just a wish. If it is more money you want, then be specific about what turnover or retained profit you want. If you want to have more free time, then be specific. "I want to spend more time with my family" is not a specific goal, again it's a wish or a hope. However, saying that you want to have every second Friday off so you can have a long weekend with your kids is a goal. It is specific and measurable and if we get this planning process right (and you read the rest of the book) then a goal like that also becomes very achievable. Set some goals, specific ones for your business right now. It's okay if you are struggling a little, things may become clearer for you as you progress through the book. If you are struggling, simply write down the first few specific goals that come to mind.

It's okay if they change over time. In fact, I always work through one of these planning sheets each 90 days with all of our Mastermind members and their twelve month goals often change. More often than not I see not so much a change in the goals but more of a refinement, they become even more specific. That's what working through this planning exercise and the rest of the exercises in the book, is designed to do for you, to give you greater clarity.

Next step is to move to the bottom left quarter. This is where we are going to get specific on the steps you need to take, the things you need to work on in order to achieve your goals. If the twelve month goals were your "what" you want to achieve to get to your "why" then this quadrant is your "how".

What you want to do here is to choose some projects that you will work on in the next 90 days which, if completed, will get you to your twelve month goals. It is important to remember here that this is not where you list the individual actions you need to take, that will come later. Here we are simply listing the projects you need to tackle in order to get to your goals. We are diving deeper into detail and at the same time we are reducing the time frame. Let's say that one of your twelve month goals was to spend one day a week going fishing instead of working in your business. In that case a project you would need to work on would be the tasks that you currently perform to see what can be delegated or removed from your schedule in order to free that day up. Once you had that as a project then the next one may be to train someone to take responsibility for something you currently do so that it can be effectively delegated. So, these are projects which will be your focus over the next 90 days. Remember you don't need to go into great detail here, just to name the project. The detail of the steps you need to take to achieve each project will come next.

Take a few minutes now and have a look at your goals. Determine three to five projects you think you can focus on in the next 90 days and write them into the projects quadrant. Don't get caught up on which ones should come first, just make sure the projects you choose align with the twelve month goals.

In this case making a start on any aligned project is better than not starting at all, so don't overthink it.

If you are struggling though here is another little tool which may help. Have a look at our Five Drivers Sheet:

The 5 Drivers

 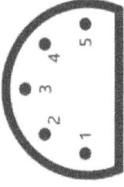  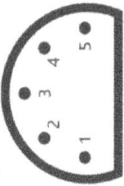 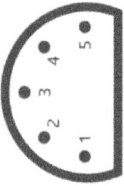

Driver: _____ Driver: _____ Driver: _____ Driver: _____ Driver: _____

Projects

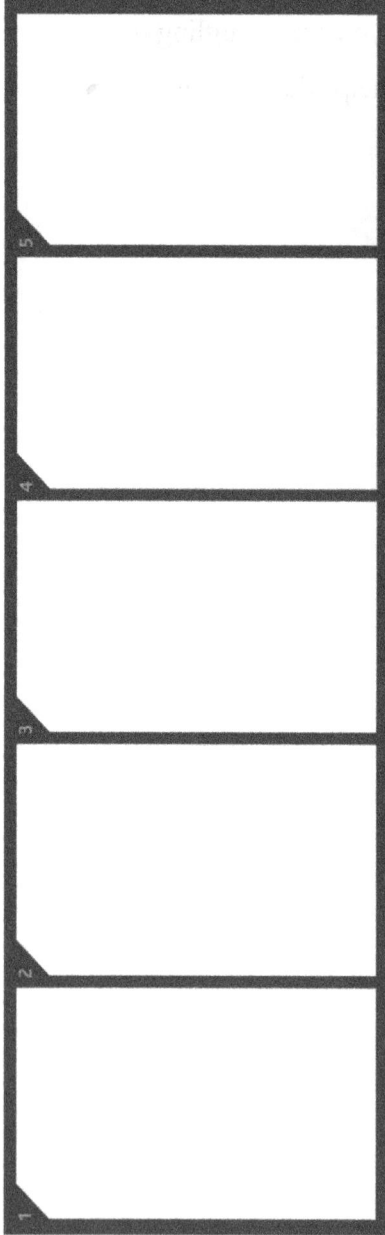

HOW

The purpose of the Five Drivers sheet is to help you gain clarity on what it is that drives you in your business. We will refer to this tool on a number of occasions throughout this book. It is a very useful tool that has quite a few applications.

Here, what we can use the Five Drivers for, is to give you clarity on your projects. So, look at your twelve month goals and list the five things that you will need to focus on in order to achieve the goals. For example, if a couple of your goals were to have that day off a fortnight and let's say to increase your retained profit by a certain dollar value. In that situation your focus areas would be time management, increasing sales and perhaps decreasing costs. So, using the Five Drivers sheet you would write in the first dial, time management and in the second dial, you would put sales generation and then in the third dial you would put costs. Now in each of those cases you can then mark on the dial on a score out of 5 where 1 is lowest and 5 is highest, how you think you currently perform. If these are areas which you need to improve on, as they clearly would be then you are not going to score yourself a 5. And if you are brutally honest, remember the only person you're fooling otherwise is you, then you are probably at a two (or maybe lower).

NOW DRAW A NEEDLE ON THE DIAL TO REFLECT YOUR SCORE FOR EACH.

The next step is to think about what are the things you need to do to move that needle on the dial. In the space under each dial list some things you need to address to move the needle. Finally, select a couple of these items from each section under the dials and they become the projects to put into your Mastermind One Page Plan. Voila! Now you have, not only a list of projects to focus on in the next 90 days but you will also have greater clarity on what will drive the improvements in your business.

Finally, we can move to the last quadrant of the One Page Plan. Now this is quite ingenious. Remember how I said at the start of this chapter that I like to keep things as simple as possible when it comes to planning. Well here's the kicker! In the last quadrant you simply make a note of the tasks you are going to do on a weekly basis in order to complete the projects from the left hand quadrant. The true beauty lies though in the fact that if you print your plan on an A4 page, the quadrants are the exact size of a rectangular Post It Note. This means that you can print the One Page Plan and simply update it weekly across each 90 day period by using post it notes for your weekly actions. There are a couple of points here. Firstly, I encourage you to keep the action steps limited to no more than five. It means that you can stay focused on those actions and not fall into overwhelm. It also allows you to focus on one thing at a time. I know we all like to think that we can multitask, but I am yet to see a truly effective multitasker in business. Note I said in business before all the mums and dads out there write to tell me about how they have to multitask on a daily basis. I read some research recently which suggested that trying to multitask on a daily basis in your work life can reduce your productivity by as much as 40%. Having a few set action plans to focus on each week will allow you to set dedicated time for them and focus on them one at a time. That way you will be functioning at a productivity rate much higher than 60%.

Secondly, get into the habit of producing these Post It actions each Monday. In Mastermind it's what we call Post It Monday. In fact, a number of our Mastermind tribe members use this within departments in their business as well. I recently went to a management meeting in a client's business and all the managers brought to the Monday morning meeting was their Post It note.

Focusing on these simple action steps each week will get your projects completed. Remember to allocate dedicated time in your calendar to perform the actions or you will get to the end of the week and not have achieved the tasks.

All that is left to do now is repeat the process each 90 days. By the time the twelve months is up, you should have advanced your business to exactly where you wanted it to be.

There is no need to copy these worksheets, they will all be available for download at *www.haveabusinessnotajob.com*

"The best way to predict the future is to create it"

Peter Drucker

THE EVER ELUSIVE BALANCE

Planning for a successful business is just one side of the coin. Like sadness and happiness are two sides of the same coin, so is business and life.

In every plan you create for your business you must allow for balance. Spending time with those who matter most should be the greatest motivator we have for pushing forward with our business plans. That should be a central goal.

Use the Goal Generator worksheet as a tool to help you set goals for yourself and your business:

THE GOAL GENERATOR

Name: Date:

TOPIC

What's the result? A GOALS LIST which is achievable.

STEP#

1 Write down a specific goal you have.

2 Set yourself a realistic time frame to achieve it.

3 List the problems and roadblocks which may prevent you from achieving the goal. (be as negative as you like)

4 List the tools or resources you will need.

5 Use the tools and resources list to create a solution to or way around each identified problem/roadblock

6 Now write the goal together with the solution and resources. E.g. I will... and... won't stop me because...

7 Share the goal with someone who will keep you accountable and share your success.

8 Visualize how you will feel when you have achieved the goal and keep visualizing it until you do.

9 Celebrate the success and repeat for each goal.

BUSINESS
ACCELERATOR MASTERMIND

CHAPTER 4

The Power Of Product

*Ice cream isn't
ice cream.*

*Understanding your
true product.*

This next secret to learning how to scale your business is also often the most contentious when I speak about it at business events.

Now that is not because it is a contentious topic as such but more because people often have difficulty in understanding (or agreeing with) the concept. The concept is to understand the true product you sell. And where it becomes contentious is that the true product is most likely not what you think it is.

For the purposes of this chapter I am going to refer to the term "product" and it applies whether your business sells a physical product or a service. It also applies whether you have a bricks and mortar premises, whether you work from home or your business is online.

In the last chapter we examined your "why" the big picture reason for you being in business in the first place.

Once you are out in the marketplace, however, the question of "why" needs to move from you to your consumer. In other words, why would they buy from you? There are a number of parts to answering this question so let's look at each of them now.

POSITION

Firstly, it helps to understand where your product sits in the marketplace. There are three components to this, which are:

1. Demographic
2. Competition
3. Uniqueness

When considering where you sit in the marketplace you need to determine the most likely demographic. That is who is most likely to buy your product.

One way that I help my clients to answer this question is I often ask them to draw a picture and describe in great detail what their ideal client or customer looks like. That's because if you don't have complete clarity around that then any marketing you do may completely miss the mark. This process is very similar to writing your business plan and should in fact form a part of it.

You may recall in the last chapter, I said about business planning that if you don't have a very clear picture of exactly where you want your business to be and how you want it to grow than there is a good chance you will never get there.

The same is true in identifying your demographic. You must set about developing a clear picture of the ideal client or customer by considering:

- How old are they?
- Where do they live?
- Where do they work?
- What do they earn?

- What do they do when they are not working?

The questions you will have to ask yourself in this process will of course depend on your product, but whatever it may be, drill down to as refined a picture as you possibly can. In Mastermind, we call it discovering your Avatar, the perfect ideal representation of your dream client. And as always, there is a simple tool which we use in Mastermind to help us do just that. This is our Mapping Your Avatar's Hot Buttons sheet.

Before you get too daunted about this let's break it down into nice simple components. What you want to do is to identify your ideal client. Yes, you want to know the logistics mentioned above such as where do they live but you also need to dive deeper into their profile than that. What you want to know is what will drive them to purchase from you. Why will they want your product?

We know that generally people buy a product to move themselves away from pain and or toward pleasure. It's what I call taking them on a journey from problem to promise and we will come back to that concept shortly. In order to be able to convince them to buy from you then you have to give them a compelling reason. You have to appeal to their emotions and show them the transformation which your product will bring to their lives.

The first step in identifying your Avatar's hot buttons is to think about four points about them:

- What are their frustrations?
- What are their immediate needs?
- What are their future fears?
- What are their future wants or aspirations?

What you are looking to do here is to take the client on a journey. You want to show them how your product can take them away from their present and immediate situation to a better future, problem to promise. In doing so, you need to make sure that you address their immediate frustrations and show them how your product will give them what they need.

By identifying their immediate frustrations, you can target your marketing and the sales message you use to sell your product in a way which shows exactly how your product removes that frustration. Let's have a look at an example. Let's say you are a finance broker. Your ideal client will be frustrated with how long it takes to research interest rates and terms and conditions from a range of lenders. So, your marketing message tells them that is exactly what a broker does. You will do all the research so that they don't have to, giving them back time to do more important or more productive tasks. What they may have as an immediate need then will be to get finance quickly and to not have to spend hours back and forth with the bank. They want to know if they can get finance and if so, how much and they want to know that as soon as possible. So, you provide a quick and easy online calculator to help them achieve that need. Once you have addressed the frustrations and wants then you can start to take them into the future which is where you will find the fears and the aspirations. Remember the idea is to take them away from the present and into the future but it also to move them away from their fears and toward their aspirations. In other words, away from pain and toward pleasure. Let's use our finance broker example again. A future fear of a finance client might be that they get locked into an interest rate which they may not be able to afford if it varies so telling them that you can find them a very flexible loan may just allay that fear. Finally, then you can move them toward their aspirations and that is where the sales magic really happens. It is also where you need to truly understand the emotional and transformational aspect of the product you sell. We are going to have a close look at that shortly. Let's just wrap up the Avatar exercise first.

Once you have listed the four components in the Hot Button sheet there are two questions in boxes on the right hand side which you need to take a few moments to answer. Firstly, what would they be likely to Google and secondly what keeps them awake at night. Again, let's use the finance broker example. I have coached some of the very top finance brokers in Australia and getting them to take these steps is exactly what helped them achieve their industry success. So, if I am looking for a home loan, will I google finance broker? Or am I more likely to google something like "how to get the best home loan?" Getting answers to these questions will simply help you to target your product and your marketing message in the right way. It will help you in your sales conversations. Helping my clients to identify themselves as Finance Strategists rather than finance brokers moved the needle on their success dial dramatically because we realized that great clients wanted much more than just a loan, they wanted a strategy.

Take a few minutes to consider what your ideal client might look for on Google and what might keep them awake at night. Now you have a completed Mapping Your Avatar's Hot Buttons Sheet you will be able to focus your marketing and your sales conversations in a way which is far more likely to see conversions for you.

MAPPING YOUR AVATAR'S HOT BUTTONS™

The secrets of attracting your avatar is not to shout. Instead, you just need to whisper the right words in the right ear. Use this hot button map to identify the fears, frustrations, wants and aspirations of your avatar.

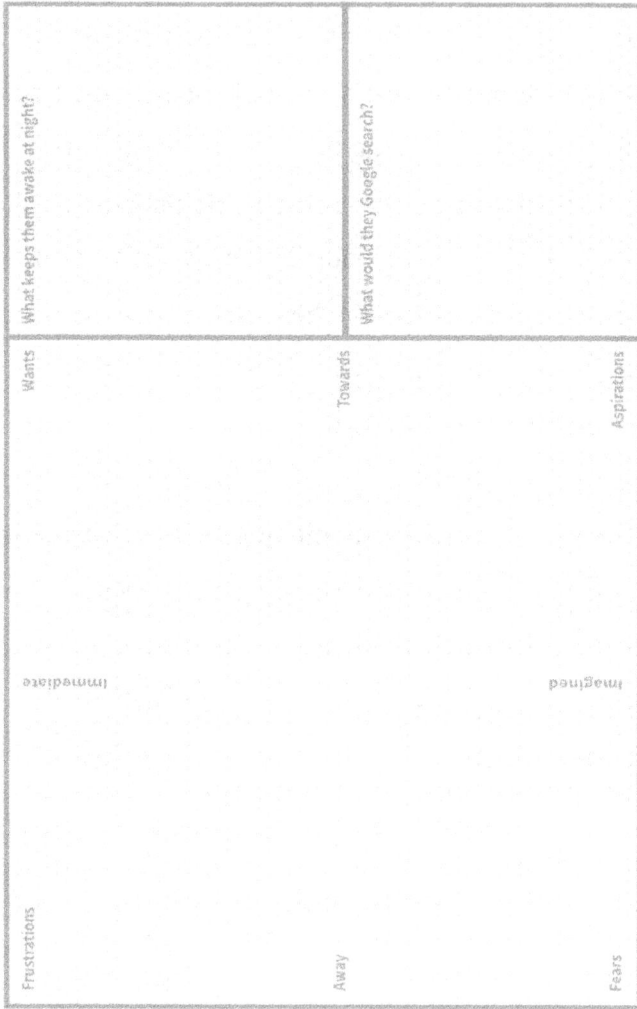

Frustrations	Wants	What keeps them awake at night?
Immediate		
Away	Towards	
		What would they Google search?
Fears	Aspirations	
Imagined		

BUSINESS
BLUEPRINT MASTERMIND

It is worth remembering that marketing is a specialised field particularly in terms of social media and I get the experts to help me in my business, so I encourage you to do the same. It was once described by my friend Michael Yardney as "a moving beast" and it continues to move at an ever increasing pace. Like anything else in business, though, there are plenty of opportunities to educate yourself and to learn as much as you can. That way you will have a greater understanding of what the experts are telling you.

Once you know where your product fits in with which demographic you need to have a look at what the competition is doing. If you retain a good marketing company, they should conduct a competitor analysis for you, but again it is well worth you staying informed as much as you can.

I always encourage my clients to take a simple two-step process

1. Review your particular industry and choose a couple of people who you admire. Generally, you will admire them for the success they have achieved and which you intend to emulate. Perhaps you admire their innovative approach to business. Whatever it is that you admire about their business, pick two or three people.

2. Spend some time finding out how they went about achieving their success. Subscribe to any information they produce. Perhaps they regularly blog or tweet. Subscribe or follow them so you can tap into their knowledge and, of course, that will also allow you to see what they are doing in the marketplace. The fact of the matter is that you cant keep up with your competition, let alone stay ahead of them, if you don't know what they are doing.

A LITTLE HINT HERE...

Whilst I always encourage clients to keep track of their competition, it doesn't always have to be in a competitive environment. If there is someone in your industry who has achieved the kind of success that you would like to and they are not in immediate direct competition to you, then as well as subscribing to anything they produce, think about asking them if you can spend some time with them.

Spending time with a competitor may seem a strange idea and it is certainly why this material is often contentious, as I warned you at the outset. The interesting thing I have found is that people are generally happy to share. If your competitor is operating their business in the same town or city and is truly an immediate competitor, they may be reluctant to give away trade secrets obviously. But, if they operate in the same industry but in a different location or perhaps appeal to a different demographic, then you may be surprised how approachable they are.

A REAL-LIFE CLIENT SUCCESS STORY

A couple of years ago I was working with a client who had achieved reasonable success in their industry but the massive growth they were hoping to achieve had escaped them.

We spent some time identifying the competitors who had achieved extraordinary growth through innovative practices. We then chose one who operated in a different State and I flew my clients to meet with the directors of the competitor.

It might be surprising to learn that those directors were very generous with their time and shared knowledge, which I am sure my clients would have discovered over time, but the conversation with the competitor allowed my clients to fast track their growth strategies. I have always found business owners who have more experience very open to sharing their knowledge so what harm is there in asking.

Is your business unique?

Now you have the skills to consider and identify your demographic and to keep an eye on your competition. The next step is to develop your own uniqueness.

You need to know the unique selling proposition (USP) of your product. In other words, what sets it apart from your competition. Elsewhere in this book I will share with you some of the secrets to developing your brand and creating a phenomenal customer experience. These may very well help you define your USP.

It's an unfortunate truth that very few businesses have the luxury of having no competition or being truly unique in the marketplace by product alone. And even if you were without competition, I wouldn't say that was necessarily a positive. Competition keeps us on our toes and innovating our business.

But back to your USP. The essential purpose of your USP is to enable you to focus your marketing and sales efforts in a way which is likely to be most effective. Do you remember how earlier in this chapter I said that the psychology would turn from the you to the consumer? This is a part of that process.

Developing your USP involves asking the question why a consumer would choose your product over that of a competitor? Your business undoubtedly means a great deal to you and you have probably put a lot of blood sweat and tears into it, which means that you may be blinded to what your customer is actually looking for. This also involves getting a true understanding of what motivates your customer to buy your product – be it from you or anyone.

Understanding the psychology of your consumer is vital to your success. In speaking with business owners I regularly hear the same myths around consumer psychology. Those myths suggest that:

- People don't care where they buy from
- Relationship selling is dead thanks to online shopping and
- Consumers are primarily driven by price.

Let me deal with each one.

Consumers are becoming smarter. It is easier now than ever before to conduct research and read online feedback on consumer experiences. It is this new smarter and better informed consumer who is now far more discerning than before.

The introduction and proliferation of online selling has actually broadened the choice for consumers so they can make sure there is an exact match to their needs more easily. They no longer have to accept anything less than exactly what they are looking for because they know they can research and most likely find, an exact match to their needs and desires.

While it may be true that face-to-face relationships are harder to come by, the concept of a consumer experience is very much alive and well. This means that the consumers of your product are looking for an experience. They want to know that you have taken an interest in them and their needs when you have designed, developed and marketed your product.

The adage that people buy people not products is still very much alive today. If that were not the case then sport and movie stars would never be able to command six figure endorsement deals would they?

And finally, there is ample consumer behaviour research to suggest that price is rarely the primary motivator behind a decision whether to purchase. No doubt if you are operating in the mass market discount space then price is your biggest consideration, but for the vast majority of small business that is simply not the case. Think about it, if price alone was the determining factor then we would all be driving Indian or Chinese cars and luxury brands in any industry would be a thing of the past. Trust me, they are not.

Now that we know what isn't true, what is? Well, we know that people buy something because it fills a need, removes a frustration, or answers a question. The job for your business in developing your USP is to get a good understanding of what that need, frustration, or question is.

Taking the time to stand in your customers' shoes is a great way to identify your USP. If you were your customer, what would compel you to buy your product? And I do mean compel because anything short of a compelling reason just leaves you alongside your competitors.

Here is another hint though...

Having a USP does not mean having a unique product. It means you need to deliver your product with a unique advantage. That advantage may be the way you deliver the product, the value-add services you provide, the personal level of your service, your guarantee or, communication. Whatever it may be, make it yours. Own that unique advantage and then shout about it at every opportunity.

The next aspect to consider is the true nature of your product from your consumers' perspective. The most successful businesses I have worked with have excelled at this aspect of their product knowledge.

When you hear about product knowledge perhaps your thoughts go to technical knowledge and whether you are in retail or a service industry there is no doubt that technical knowledge is invaluable.

There can be nothing more frustrating as a consumer than dealing with a business where the owner or staff don't actually know exactly what the product is. It is actually one of my pet hates when I go to a restaurant and ask the wait staff about a dish and they are not able to tell me about it in detail. Here, however, I am talking about psychological or emotional product knowledge, which can be a big stumbling block for some business owners and their staff. Let me give you some examples to make the point.

A REAL-LIFE CLIENT SUCCESS STORY

I worked with the owner of an ice cream shop some years ago. We were discussing the product one day and he mentioned the 30 or so flavours, the different cones and the three different types of hot fudge sauce. And that, he said was the product, that is what people came to his store for.

I went through the process of asking him what he thought was going on for his customers when they came to his store. Ice cream is not a staple food, I said, so consumers don't go to an ice cream store because they need feeding or because they need that particular "nutrition". So, I asked him what mood people were in when they came to the store. After some discussion he realised that people came to buy ice cream essentially with three different emotions. They bought ice cream when they were happy and wanted to spend time with friends treating themselves, when they were celebrating a nice night out and finishing with a treat of ice cream, or when they were feeling like they needed to be cheered up and ice cream was the answer.

The end result of that discussion was my client realised that ice cream was a treat which delivered happiness. The product he was selling was therefore happiness. And this is where I sometimes get resistance.

Understanding the emotional aspect of your product will not only help you to stand out from your competition but it will also help you to tailor your business growth strategy. Let me explain further…

Once my ice cream parlour client knew the emotional aspect of his product he changed his staff training and customer service practices. Rather than focusing on getting the customer to choose a flavour, he trained his staff to engage with the customer around what brought them to the store. Staff started asking customers what they were celebrating, where they had been before coming to the ice cream shop and even started hearing stories of breakups and ice cream for commiseration. Guess what happened then?

As a result, customers enjoyed the experience, were even happier inside the store and sales increased. Up-selling to larger scoops, extra fudge and waffle cones happened on almost every sale. My client increased his turnover by 25 percent. But wait, there's more. More customers joined the loyalty program and he had less staff turnover. The experience became a positive one for all involved. I remember when my daughter Samantha was a teenager and she would break up with a boyfriend, the ice cream shop is where we would go. There she could console her broken heart with ice cream and I could celebrate that she moved on from a boy I didn't like anyway!

So, using this ice cream analogy, understanding the emotional aspect of your product can bring similar results in your business. I worked with a pool shop a couple of years ago and the same thing happened. Once I was able to help the client to see that the true product was expertise and not pool chemicals, then they were also able to increase their sales. Customers took the advice from the pool shop staff and product sales increased.

Interestingly, though, not only did they increase in-store sales, but customers started asking for pool servicing as well, all because the staff started to sell the advice and the lifestyle aspect of the product. They became emotionally in-tune with their customer so selling a lifestyle convenience product such as pool servicing became exceptionally easy.

So, ice cream is about happiness, pool chemicals are about expertise and lifestyle. What is the emotional aspect of your product? Spend some time determining that and you will find that increased sales or easier sales conversions will follow. This is where we can close the loop. Once you understand the emotional or transformational aspect of your product then you can apply that knowledge to your earlier Avatar exercise. How will your product bring transformation to your Avatar? Given that you have identified the fears, frustrations, needs and aspirations of your ideal client, consider how your new found knowledge of the emotional transformation of your product can meet those Avatar points. Using the earlier finance broker example, we discovered that the emotional transformation which finance broking products bring were freedom, choices, the ability to buy that dream home or secure the future with an investment property. Using that knowledge, we transitioned our broker clients to finance strategists which in turn allowed them to provide advice which allayed the fears, removed the frustrations, met an immediate need and helped achieve a future aspiration. And it became so much easier than trying to sell a loan. Who wakes up in the morning, has a look at a beautiful day outside and says " I think I will go and borrow several hundreds of thousands of dollars which will put me in debt for the next 25 years"? No one of course, it is just a matter of determining the true product and then the message becomes clear.

The other great thing is that once you understand the Avatar Hot Button concept, have it clearly mapped and are able to clearly state the transformational emotional aspect of your product you will find a shift from having to "sell" to needing merely to send the right message to the right audience and your clients will "buy". I have seen that very transformation happen with many of our Mastermind clients.

The final secret I want to share with you around your product is to consider innovation. If you have been in business for some time perhaps you identified your USP a while ago or maybe you only identified it recently. If you are just starting up, you may have determined your USP from looking at your competitors.

Whichever the case, the final step you need to take is to keep innovating. Constantly review your USP, continually train your staff in the emotional aspect of your product and always keep an eye on the competition.

Longevity in business comes from constantly reviewing what you do, finding ways to improve and being open to new challenges, idea and innovative solutions.

Let's move on to the next chapter, where we'll learn about branding...

CHAPTER 5

You Better Understand Branding

"Your brand is what other people say about you when you are not in the room"

Jeff Bezos

The first thing I need to say before I share this secret with you is that I am not a marketing consultant. I don't have a marketing degree and I have never worked in marketing.

Now that we have that clarity, let' talk about what I can share with you. As a business coach I work with some of the best and most successful entrepreneurs in Australia. I've watched them take their personal and company brands to great heights and I have seen them build very successful businesses through very clever and strategic marketing campaign. It is that clever strategic thinking that I am about to share with you.

In this chapter we are going to consider how you build your brand, how you get your buying customer to understand your product or service and then the very simple ways that you can spread the word and attract business.

Know the good and the bad

One of the first things I have a new coaching client do is to complete a SWOT analysis (there is a simple template at the end of this book) not only of their business but of them personally. There are a number of reasons for this and I also address some of them elsewhere in this book in the chapter on the secret to attracting and managing great people in your business.

Firstly, from a brand development perspective, it is important to recognise that we each have a personal brand. Understanding this will enable you to separate yourself from your business when you need to and that is the secret to longevity. It will allow you to develop a succession plan, an exit strategy and give you the opportunity to develop a true legacy with your business.

Perhaps, like me initially, you are your business. If you are in a service industry, you generate the business, do the work, perform the role of the bookkeeper (in which case you need to study my secret to financial management chapter in this book) and everything in between, then the idea that there can be essentially two brands within your business will be unthinkable.

But even in that scenario, if you start to outsource roles within your business and leverage off your knowledge and expertise you can start to develop scalable products which have a separate identity. It is the only way you can manufacture "goodwill value". Otherwise the business is just you and therefore without you it has no intrinsic value. Still not convinced? Let's look at an example.

STEVE THE ACCOUNTANT

Take the example of a sole practice accountant. Let's call him Steve. Steve has a small accounting practice, which consists of himself and one support person. He meets with the clients, performs the accounting work and generates the accounts. He is it. There is only one brand, Brand Steve. Not so however. Let's imagine that Steve starts to produce some simple tip sheets and develops an online presence where business people can start to get online tips on small business accounting. Steve then teams up with a local bookkeeper and runs some podcasts or webinars. That online presence starts to gather momentum and its own database outside of Steve's clients.

Suddenly Steve has two brands, Steve the Accountant and Online Steve. If he is clever about how he develops the online presence and starts to monetise it then he has a tangible asset which, over time, may very well become valuable quite independent of his brand. If Steve then creates clever strategic alliances, which I will talk about later in this chapter, then his online brand can take on a whole independent identity.

Now, of course, that online presence will also start to refer clients to Steve the Accountant, which in turn adds value to his personal brand. The important thing here is that it gives Steve options for the future.

MICHAEL THE ENTREPRENEUR

One of my very successful entrepreneur clients, Michael Yardney, has done exactly that. He has the Michael Yardney Brand, which is involved heavily in educating people around wealth creation through property and together with his business partners he has developed another successful brand in Metropole Property Strategists.

They work hand in glove but are very separate identities. Michael has been able to take the concept one step further and through partnerships use his own personal brand to create other businesses which use his personal brand to generate interest and leads. It is very clever and, came about as a result of a lot of strategic thinking and hard work over a number of years, but it is achievable for anyone.

Do you know brand rules?

We know that the world is changing rapidly and what worked five years ago may no longer be relevant. Consumers are bombarded on a daily basis with a never-ending stream of messages all vying for their consumer dollar.

So, in light of this new reality, here are some simple steps you can take to get your brand ready to compete in that very competitive landscape:

Answer the question " why?". Why are you in business? What is your central purpose? This is a time to be brutally honest with yourself. You may think that the most common answer would be "to make money" but in fact in my experience it isn't. My clients see money as the biproduct of what they do. It is the reward for being in business but by no means is it their reason or their "why". You see, money comes and goes and it is really just a commodity. It is a nice commodity to have and life is a whole lot easier with than without it, but it won't provide you with a central purpose. Maybe you are in business to help people, maybe it's to change perceptions, or maybe it is as simple as that you want to achieve status or have a professional qualification. Hopefully you are in business because you love it and it is your passion.

The clients I enjoy working with are those who run their business because it is their passion. When I coached Katrina Christ, arguably Australia's leading family portrait photographer, I was always impressed with her commitment to her passion. The business therefore became an extension of that passion and so growth became relatively easy.

As with many of the secrets contained in this book, though, a word of caution… just because you have a passion does not guarantee success in turning that passion into a business. It is of course an amazing and often essential ingredient, but even in our new disruptive, digital world nothing replaces commitment, drive, determination and strategic hard work. Luck can play a part but as one of my longest serving clients says, it took him 20 years to be an overnight success.

One you've answered why you are in business you need to use that answer to create the story. This is the "who". Who are you? By now you have clarity around why you run your business but what do you answer when someone asks what you do?

A simple exercise I use with my clients is to say, if you met someone at a social function on the weekend and they asked what you did, how would you answer? At first glance this seems like an easy straightforward question to answer. But what if I asked you to answer in a way which compelled the person to want to know more, to engage with you in a longer conversation all about you and your business, or even better still to actually buy your product or services?

This is where the distinction between your passion and your story become relevant. If someone asks you what you do and your answer is not compelling it is more than likely that they will never get to hear about how passionate you are. The answer to the "what" question needs to be immediately compelling. It needs to be infused with your passion and it needs to beg the very next comment to be "tell me more".

MARK THE BUSINESS COACH

I consider myself to be extremely fortunate. I love what I do and I get to do what I love for a living. Clients pay me substantial sums of money to coach them, which is my passion.

I get to mix with entrepreneurs and I constantly learn from my clients as well. What a dream job! But let me ask you this. If you met me socially and asked what I did for a living and I answered "Business Coach" would you stay around to ask another question? It's OK to be honest, I can't hear you.

You see if I answered that way I would never get to tell you about my passion, how working with my clients and seeing people achieve their dreams and goals is what motivates me, or how seeing my clients go through very real personal change, which has an amazing positive impact on their business is what gets me out of bed every day.

I wouldn't get to tell you how speaking at industry events across Australia and internationally is a huge buzz for me or how having a client tell me that I have changed their life is enough of a reward that I would do it for no money at all. I also wouldn't get to tell you how being paid allows me to give back, to make a positive contribution to the business community, to mentor young business owners who simply couldn't afford my fees. And to contribute to my community and society at large in the hope that I can leave this world just a little better than it is now - to leave a legacy for my grandchildren.

I wonder if you would get that chance when you are asked that question? That is why I encourage all of my clients to develop and practice their story so that they end up with a clear and compelling answer to the "what" question. Remember I asked before how would you react if I told you I was a Business Coach? What if my answer to the "what" question was that I am the "unreasonable friend" to some of Australia's leading entrepreneurs? Would that make you ask more?

So how will you answer? How will you infuse your answer with your passion? I recently met a jeweller who described himself as a pleaser of women, using diamonds! And what about the portrait photographer who describes her photography as capturing family memories? How compelling is that? Take some time to think about your story, practice it and fine tune it until you get that wow factor which compels someone to say, "that's interesting, tell me more".

Finally, once we have the "what" and "why" answered we can focus on the how. This is about developing strategies to get your brand out into the marketplace. I'm not going to talk about marketing and I'm certainly not going to tell you the secrets of social media. But I will encourage you to get an understanding of it. Social media is undoubtedly here to stay and will also undoubtedly change and develop rapidly.

I recently attended a Roger Hamilton seminar where it was stated that there would be more developments in technology in the next five years than in the past 20. The industrial age is undoubtedly finished and there is a new world order particularly in the online and social media space. It is now a specialised field and one in which I also take advice from specialists. What I will talk about now, however, is tried and true strategies for getting your brand, both the brand of your business and your personal brand into the big wide world.

I encourage all of my clients to spread the word of their brand at every available opportunity. Kevin Turner, one of the most influential people in Australian real estate media often says you never know who you are standing next to. So whoever it may be, seize the opportunity to tell them who you are, what you do and why.

If you have it confidently developed, then your enthusiasm will be infectious. In another chapter, I will talk more about establishing strategic alliances and how that can effectively develop your brand presence.

The fourth rule is simply to be authentic. Even though the world is faster paced than ever before, the digital age has meant that consumers are also far better educated. Researching you on the web is easy and if the story you tell, doesn't match what people read about you online then you are wasting your time. Just as importantly, though, having a business and therefore a brand that you can wholeheartedly support - and one which represents your values and ideals - is so much easier for you to believe in , to support and commit toand to make the sacrifices which we all have to make as our business grows.

Being authentic will attract the right people. Whether it be as consumers or as team members, it will also drive loyalty to your brand, something which is essential even today. If the brand you have developed is not representative of the goals and purpose you have set for yourself then you have a lack of congruency and the operation of your business may ultimately become a burden. Take some time out to look at your brand and make sure you have met these rules. If you haven't, change it now, set about creating a new story, the one which best reflects you.

CHAPTER 6

The Business Of People

*"If you think it's expensive to hire a professional....
wait until you hire an amateur"*
Red Adair

Now that we've covered off on understanding your product as well as your brand, in this chapter I am going to share with you the importance of people in your business. Sounds obvious, doesn't it? I am constantly surprised, however, at business owners who fail to understand the importance of people and relationships for their business. To prevent such a thing happening to you and your business, though, I am going to show you how to get the very best from the people around you.

We will look at areas of:

- Recruitment
- Motivation
- Training
- Delegation and
- Culture

What if you don't have staff, or your business is in its very early stages and it is just you? Perhaps it's a family business of just you and your partner. Please don't skip this thinking it won't apply to or help you. If your business grows (and that is probably why you are reading this book after all) then understanding this information will put you in a strong position to take on the right staff at the right time.

Even if you have no intention of taking on staff and you propose to outsource all the support you need, then what is about to follow in the next few pages will give you insight as well. You see, no matter how digital or disruptive business becomes, there is still an underlying need for contact and connection between human beings. That is, until such time as artificial intelligence can produce automated robotic support to take the place of humans. I know it is developing and I am sure an edition of this book in 20 years' time will be very different, but in the foreseeable future understanding human behaviour and having strong people management skills will still contribute significantly to your success. Even if your business is just you and your partner, these skills will improve the efficiency of your business.

RECRUITMENT

Recruitment is a specialised field. After all, it is a whole university degree in itself. If you are running a larger organisation you probably have a recruitment manager or human resources person as a part of your full-time staff. If you don't, then, it is something you should consider, but I will come back to that a little later.

There is a saying in recruitment which is "hire slow and fire fast". It's a nice theory but not so applicable given the various laws around fair work and unfair dismissal practices. Even without those laws, however, I think it is a bit of an antiquated business practice. The concept of hiring slow I agree with and we will look at that shortly, however, the fire fast fails to take account of the importance of properly managing your team.

THE TRUTH ABOUT HIRING

One of the most common mistakes I see in small business is the owner hiring someone because they like them. The second most common is hiring someone because they are just like you.

Bringing a staff member into your business has to be a part of an overall strategic plan for your business growth. And so your decision also has to be strategic. Hiring someone because you like them may seem a good idea at the time. Why not? At least it will be someone you can get along with, there probably won't be any workplace conflict and you can have someone you can communicate easily with.

Now, before we get too critical of that thinking, there are aspects of it that make sense. It can be lonely in small business. I have coached owners and CEO's of businesses, which range from husband and wife with no employees up to businesses with 200 staff. A common thread across all of those businesses is that it can be very lonely at the top. So, employing someone who you like and who you think you might get on well with does make some sense. Not to mention that fact that as an employee you probably spend more time with your work colleagues than you do with your family - and as a business owner that is even more so.

On that basis, liking your staff can make sense. The problem is that it isn't very strategic. Liking an employee is fine as a factor, particularly in a small environment, but it cannot and should not be the determining factor.

So how do you choose someone to work with you in your business?

I will give you some simple steps to follow but you should also think about the language I just used, finding someone to work with you as opposed to for you. That is a great factor to keep in mind, but let's look at some easy to follow steps first:

1. Conduct a quick SWOT analysis of yourself and identify your weaknesses. Keep those in mind when you are looking to recruit. Depending on the role and we will come to that, you want to find someone who will compliment your skill set as opposed to duplicating it.

2. Conduct a SWOT analysis of the business. Again, identify the weaknesses and design a role which will best fill that gap for you. Have a look at your opportunities as you may be able to design a role which addresses a weakness but can also take advantage of an opportunity (if you need some guidance there is a simple SWOT template and guide at the back of this book).

3. Be absolutely clear around the role you are looking to fill. Take some time to look at your business plan and goals and think clearly about what role will accelerate you toward those goals.

Too often I see small business owners almost hit the panic button as their growth starts to accelerate and they simply hire someone to try and take some pressure off only to find they didn't hire the right person. In most cases that will be because they either did not take the time to clearly define the role or once they have taken someone on, they have been very poor at delegating any of their tasks. We will talk about that shortly as well.

4. Commit to writing down the expectations you have of your new team member, but you must be clear and detailed. Many of the disputes and issues I see come about largely from a lack of clarity around expectations. This can be partly addressed with a position description but that just addresses the expectations around the tasks themselves. Be clear on what your expectations are regarding attitude, commitment and cultural perspective as well. I will share some more secrets around building a great culture with you shortly.

5. Finally, hire for culture more than skills. This may seem like a strange idea. Surely you need someone

with specific skills. Generally speaking, as long as a candidate has the basic skills you need, which you will have identified by following the previous steps, then you will be able to train them and fine-tune their skills to best meet the needs of your business.

What you won't be able to do is change a candidate's basic personality traits and if they are not a culture fit for your business it is not going to end well for either of you. I really can't stress this point enough. I have seen great businesses become terribly embroiled in conflict simply because of a poor culture fit of just one employee. If you don't know what your culture is, I will show you how to define that shortly.

HOW'S THE MOTIVATION?

I often have small business owners say that they wish they could have their staff as committed to the business as they are. My answer is always the same. Firstly, if they were as completely committed as you to your business there is a good chance they would be running their own business.

As a business owner you know that you think differently from most employees. If you didn't, then, you may very well still be an employee and not have taken the leap of faith into your own business.

Secondly, I ask what they are doing to motivate their employees to get them more involved and more committed.

There can be a happy balance here but it won't come from wishing for it.

Here is a simple analogy I like to use. If I were to come to your home in my car and ask you to get in and come for a drive with me, what is the most likely first question you would ask? It's probably, "Where are we going?", which is not an unreasonable question. It is certainly the one I would ask. And yet business owners do exactly the opposite on a daily basis.

They expect their employees to get in the car (their business) and travel to who knows where (the destination/goals) without ever actually sharing either the destination or the real purpose of the journey. And then they wonder why their team are not as committed as they are!

Now that we have the analogy, let's look at what you can do in your business to address the problem by following some simple steps.

1. *Hold regular meetings.* I am not one for meetings just for the sake of a meeting, but I always encourage my clients to have a meeting with their entire team at least every six months. The purpose of that meeting is to share the journey.

I often talk about the importance of having clear goals set and to review them at six-month intervals. Use that review time to share with your team. There may be aspects of your goals, personal or financial goals that you would prefer not to share and that's fine, but at least share the vision.

Tell your team what you all have achieved together over the past six months and where you want to see the business in the next six months. You may just be surprised at how your team will step up and start working with greater commitment to that goal.

2. *Celebrate the wins.* When you achieve a goal or a milestone or have an unexpected win in your business, celebrate it and include your team in those celebrations. In my business when we secure a new client, we celebrate as a team. It doesn't have to be anything extravagant. A lunch or even a morning tea if you are all in the one location. If you are geographically spread then even a hand delivered bottle of wine, gourmet basket or even a lottery ticket just to let them know that you value the contribution they have made to your business. You could take the view that your employees are getting paid so why should you do any more for them and to some degree you may be right, but I am yet to see a business with that approach reach its true potential.

3. *Thank them.* I know that seems basic and obvious but let me share a story with you.

CARL THE GENERAL SALES MANAGER

I was coaching a large car dealership and the dealer principal asked me to spend some time with the General Sales Manager of one of the brands. Let's call him Carl. The manager was a pretty likeable, affable kind of guy and had been managing a sales department for about five years. His sales figures were pretty good but he was working very long hours, constantly having to monitor and micro-manage his sales team. His stress levels were high and he was taking a good deal of that home to his wife and young son.

When we drilled down into his daily practices, he told me that every morning he would have to remind his sales team to unlock the cars, put the prices on the windscreen, as well as the flags out. Each morning he would arrive at work early and his team would turn up right on the dot of 8am. Then he would have to push them all day and it was exhausting. He told me that he ran the team that way until either he broke and fired someone, or they broke and quit.

I asked him when the last time was he thanked the team for their day's work and when was the last time he shared some celebration around wins with them rather than just riding them on figures. The answer to both was a resounding " never".

"I don't need to thank them," he said. " They get well paid to do their job; they just need to do it."

So, I tasked this sales manager with thanking his team at the end of each day. I wanted him to make a conscious effort to thank each and every one of his team individually for their efforts that day. I will admit he did resist but agreed to trial my strategy for two weeks.

Each day he thanked them. I also tasked him with having a quick power meeting once each week where he would share the wins from the previous week and the vision for the following week. The rules were simple. It had to be a quick meeting of no more than 15 minutes. It had to be positive, no negative comments allowed (they could be delivered privately and one-on-one if needed) and it had to share the vision he had for the department.

What do you think happened? Within just two weeks, the attitude of the majority of the team changed. He started arriving at work to find some of the team already there. Cars were unlocked without being directed, prices were on windscreens and flags were also out. Equally importantly, though, sales increased and over the following three months sales continued to increase.

He now had a team which was committed to the cause, partly because they now knew exactly what the cause was and partly because they felt valued and appreciated. This is exactly what I referred to at the beginning of this chapter.

No matter how automated we are becoming, we still have to deal with human beings. And with that brings human emotion. Whether people are internally or externally motivated they still need to be valued, it is a basic human desire. So, his sales team was now happier, more motivated, valued and appreciated and it showed in their interaction with customers which in turn led to increased sales.

Now this isn't a fairy tale, there wasn't a happy ending for everyone. A few of his team didn't change and so they either felt completely out of place and quit or he had to dismiss them because their sales figures didn't change either. The good news was that he was now replacing people for the right reasons and he was developing a team culture that was infectious. In fact, when he moved on to a more senior position at another dealership, the culture he had established lived on and does so to this day.

To motivate your team, take the simple steps set out above and watch the changes happen. If you'd like to know whether your team are internally or externally motivated there is a resource available for download at www.haveabusinessnotajob.com which you can have them complete. It will help you to manage and understand how to keep them motivated.

INCENTIVES

We hear regularly that to motivate people you have to incentivize them. Invariably we think that means throwing money at them. Sure, some people are motivated by money but as Daniel Pink explains in his book Drive, money alone is rarely a good motivator. In fact, according to Daniel's research and many scholarly articles he quotes, monetary incentives can actually have the opposite effect and demotivate people.

It is an interesting conundrum but as a Coach I have seen plenty of situations where business owner or department manager will put in place a financial bonus for performance only to be totally dismayed at the end of the month that no one in the team has stepped to claim the prize.

Getting to know the people who contribute to your business, whether they are staff in house, contractors, out sourced or even off shore team members, will help enormously. A little like the car analogy above, once we get to know them and understand what is driving them then we can do our best to make sure that the work you provide and the culture you establish is designed to align with their motivation.

Simple steps like asking what motivates them and what their future plans are. I always encourage our Mastermind clients to use the tools like The One page Plan and the Five Dials dashboard to help their team gain better clarity on what they are looking for, how they think they will get there and what they need to focus on. Getting to understand this aspect of your team will help you to get them:

1. More engaged
2. More committed
3. More passionate

Now, don't get me wrong financial incentives still have a place, otherwise we would all work for free! The trick is to not make the financial incentive the only tool in your arsenal. As Daniel Pink says, the three things we need to provide team members in order to get the very best from them is:

1. Autonomy
2. Mastery
3. Purpose

Spending time creating autonomy for your team, allowing them to master their role and to take both pride in it and responsibility for it. Understanding that through gather work they are seeking a sense of purpose will take you a long way towards having a motivated and incentivized team. If you want a detailed examination of this have a read of Daniel Pink's book Drive. To get started on the process though take the following steps:

AUTONOMY

Set about understanding the key drivers in your business and the structure you have around each driver. I always work on the following:

- Sales
- Financial management
- Operational management
- Team
- Leadership

Establish a clear structure within your business for each of those drivers, or the five drivers you have identified by completing the Five Dials exercise

1. Create simple yet effective systems for each of the structures around your five drivers.
2. Allocate responsibility for the systems
3. Put in place management and exception reporting protocols (more about exception reporting in the section on delegation)
4. Allow those taking responsibility for a system to review it and suggest better or more efficient ways of doing things.

Following these five simple steps will give your team members a level of autonomy, self-governance which in turn will provide them with motivation and in itself act as an incentive for them to perform at a higher level.

Mastery

Helping your team to master their skills may just be the best investment you can make in your business. Remember the whole idea is to create a scalable business which is less reliant on you actually having to be involved in the day to day operations. Here too, there is a simple step you can take to achieve that goal:

INVEST IN TRAINING

When was the last time you invested in training your team (even a team of one employee)? Elsewhere in this book I talk about the importance of innovation and, of staying relevant. You need to be constantly reviewing your product, service delivery and how you communicate with your customers and clients. That same innovation mantra applies equally to the people inside your business.

Have you ever dealt with a business and received bad service? It is interesting because if I ever ask that question at seminars or keynote speaking engagements. I am overwhelmed with a resounding yes! What about great service? When was the last time you received that?

However, let's get back to your poor service experience. When you get poor service or a bad customer experience do you blame the person delivering it? If you are like the majority of the population, the answer would be yes. And sometimes that is appropriate, but in a good number of cases, that poor service experience can be traced back to poor training by the business owner.

If you currently have a business, how much training of your team do you do? Staying competitive in business requires constant innovation, which is why I mention it so often in this book. But your business can't be truly innovative if you aren't committing time and resources to keeping your team innovative as well. Training your team can easily be pushed aside as it competes with everything else you have to do in your business. Here are some simple steps I encourage my clients to follow to improve training in your business.

1. Make a list of the areas you want your team trained in. I always focus on areas such as:
   a. Customer service
   b. Communication
   c. Product knowledge
   d. Technical skills
   e. Management skills (for those in management roles)

2. Set up a timetable for the coming 12 months and allocate dedicated time for staff training. Where possible get the team involved either through one-on-one consultation or by holding a team meeting with the specific agenda of designing the team training. Remember the more buy-in you get to the training, the more likely they are going to want to participate and the more they will get from it.

3. Remember that adults learn and retain more when they are having fun, so try to include some fun elements to the process.

Once you have the topics and the schedule, lock it in and make it happen. If budget permits, engage someone to help you with the training. Your team may hear the same thing you have been saying for some time but take greater notice just because they are hearing from a different voice.

As a coach, I hear that all the time. When I start working with the management team in a business, the directors will often comment that they have been asking a manager to do a certain thing or to do it a certain way for some time, but when they hear it from me they do it.

I know that can be frustrating but it is a bit of a phenomenon, so my advice is, don't fight it and, find a way to work with it. There are some excellent team trainers available and the cost is often very reasonable. Do some research and see what is available to you and what is a good match for your training schedule.

Remember not to just focus on technical skills. Training your people in the "soft" skills such as communication and customer service will reap rewards for your business.

If you have a sales environment and a dedicated sales team, ask them to conduct some sales training for the non-sales team. Remember anyone who has a customer-facing role is in sales so a few extra skills will never hurt. In fact, I have seen quite dramatic results by providing the administration team with some basic sales training.

Finally, two things: Don't treat training as a necessary evil. It ought to be a part of the proactive management of your business. Helping your team to reach their potential in your business can only benefit you. The benefits come from your team being better skilled and providing superior service to your customers and it is also likely to increase your staff retention. Of course, both are excellent outcomes for your business. When I talk to clients about team training, I am often asked, "What if I spend this money on training and then they leave?" My reply is always, "What if you don't and they stay!"

PURPOSE

We all need a sense of purpose. We are, after all, human beings and not human doings. Creating a sense of purpose for the people in your business can be a real challenge. What if their role is mundane, never changing and routine? Well the good news is that there are two ways you can address the purpose issue. Let's have a look at both of them.

1. Internal – purpose within your business
2. External – helping promote a purpose they have outside of work.

INTERNAL

Helping your team to develop a sense of purpose may be easier than you think. Every person in your business plays their own vital role

On the next page is a great worksheet to use with your team:

TEAM PORTRAIT™

TEAM CHARACTER

TEAM MOTTO

TEAM VISION

BUSINESS
MASTERMIND

CHAPTER 7

Culture

"I have always said, the way you treat your employees is the way they will treat your customers"

Richard Branson

You may wonder why I have included a section on culture in a book all about building a business. Remember though, the whole concept of this book is to help you to build a Level Three business, one that relies less on you, one that scales so you can spend more time on life and less time tied to the business.

To achieve that you are going to have to get good people around you, the right people. Of course, there will be many things in your business that you will be able to automate and a reasonable part of any scaling plan will include automation, employing technology rather than people. Not everything can be automated though and you are going to have to rely on other human beings, in many aspects, as your business grows.

Let's just make a little side note here - you may be thinking that you will build a business with no staff, an online venture with no bricks and mortar component and no one working for you. So, let me give you my definition of 'team'. Your team in your business is so much more than people directly employed by you. It includes contractors, offshore workers and it also includes those on whom your business relies. Think about suppliers, referral partners, sub-contractors and alliances. Here is the real twist though, what about your clients? They too, are members of your 'team'.

With that definition in mind let's look at what part culture plays and why you have to work to develop a great one. Later in this chapter I am going to show you how to develop a great team of employees and immediate workers but for this part lets focus on the role culture plays.

Building a great culture in your business will see people want to be associated with you. As human beings we are far more likely to do business with people we like and with whom we have some common values. Your values form the very cornerstone of the culture in your business. So here is a simple three step process to develop a compelling positive culture. Doing so will have the advantage of:

1. Making your business a desirable place to be on a daily basis.
2. Driving clients to you because of a sharing of common values.
3. Make you an employer of choice. Which means you will have higher retention and easier recruitment.
4. Help you to stand neck and shoulders above your competition.

Here is the three-step process:

1. Define and live your values.
2. Clarify your vision.
3. Share both.

There you go, seems pretty simple and obvious doesn't it? Let's look at each and give you some simple and practical tools for making it happen. Remember this book is all about implementation, not just theorising.

Define your Values...

Your values are the core beliefs which drive your business. When I coach people on this and I ask them for the values of their business, I more often than not receive big picture answers like honesty or integrity. I see those values as falling into the "I should bloody well hope so" category. They are really just words and in terms of values they should be a given.

Values in your business need to be more like guiding principles and to be that, you have to look more closely, dive a little deeper, into what the values mean to you. Look at what they will mean to your team (and keep in mind my extended definition of 'team') and how they will be implemented into your business so they can be lived on a daily basis.

Let me give you an example so that you can start this process for yourself. Let's say that honesty was a value that came to mind first as you were reading this. That's great news of course however, you need to dive deeper. How will that honesty be practiced? How will it apply to your team, your clients? I went through this exercise with a mastermind member recently and he said that for his business it meant that he would always be honest with his team, share with them the good news and the bad in the business. He also said that he would give his clients complete transparency, would never cover up a mistake or when something had not gone according to plan.

Here is the values statement he developed:

"We will always be completely honest with our team members and share with them both the wins and the losses in the business. Our clients will always be kept fully informed, no matter the outcome. We will never cover things up to make ourselves look better and if we make a mistake, we will own it and own up to it straight away and then work to make it right for our clients, suppliers and partners. That is the cornerstone of what we do"

Wow, what a powerful statement. Wouldn't you want to work at a business that had that as a core value? Wouldn't you want to do business with someone who practiced that as a value?

Here is a simple exercise to help you develop your own core values.

Grab a book of Post It notes. Set yourself a timer of three minutes and start writing down the things that spring to mind when you think about core values. Write one per Post it Note.

When the timer is up, spread the notes out in front of you. It doesn't matter how many you have and it doesn't matter if many are similar. In fact, if that is the case then it shows that is a predominant theme for you and something which is going to be very much at the core of what you do.

Next, set your timer for one minute and in that time take away the four values which you think are either repeated, or less important to you. Now, take a moment to look at the six you have left. How do they feel to you? Are they resonating? Can you see how they can be implemented in your business? Can you see how they might make a difference to your extended team?

Great! Now let's narrow it down just a little more. Set your timer for one minute and in that time take away two or three notes, again the ones which resonate with you the least out of the six you have in front of you. Don't over think it. You can always revisit and fine tune this as time goes on. But having a set of values which are good, if not great, is better than not having any at all!

Now, you will have three or four values left in front of you. They are the core values. They are the values that you are going to make sure your business lives by and form a part of the way you run the business on a daily basis.

The last step is to put each of them onto a statement. Again, don't let perfect be the enemy of good. Try simple statements that start with things like, "We will' or "We always". Would you like an example? Let's say you have integrity as a final core value. In that case your implementation statement might look something like this;

"We will always behave in a way which shows the utmost integrity towards everyone we do business with. We will never behave in a way which breaches that integrity, or which is even borderline. We understand that our integrity, the way we behave as a business, is at the core of our reputation and our reputation is not negotiable, ever!"

Set aside some time to complete your own value statements and then share them with everyone you do business with. If you have staff, either in your premises, working remotely or even as contractors, get then involved in the exercise. It will give them a chance to be a part of what you are building and as you will see later in this book, a sense of belonging is vital to your team members.

Once you have developed the statements, shout them from the hilltops. Wear them bravely and proudly and make them a part of your message. Finally, take the time to stop and do a reality check at regular intervals, to critically examine how you are doing at living the values.

Plus, feel free to adjust the statements as time goes on. Having these simple yet clear value statements is a step one in the process to developing a phenomenal culture. Remember not only will a great culture make people want to work with and for you, it will also make you feel pretty good about what you are doing.

___

CLARIFY YOUR VISION....

I find that business owners often confuse the concept of a vision and a mission statement. So, let me give you a simple definition that I work by. It may not be the same as you have read elsewhere and it certainly may not be the one you will read in a textbook, but it is the one which I have used to help hundreds of entrepreneurs develop for very successful businesses.

A mission is the thing you want your business to achieve at a very high level, a bit like a guiding principle with an outcome attached. An example of a mission might be something like "To positively impact the lives of twenty thousand people by 2030". As you can see it is a big picture statement. In the 1960's NASA had a mission to boldly expand frontiers in air and space. That was the big picture mission statement. The vision was to land a man on the moon. Do you see the difference?

Your vision, therefore, is where you see your business in the future. Having a clear picture, a clear understanding of the vision of the business, will help you to ensure that you are tracking correctly. It can serve as a constant reminder for the reason behind the hard yards and as a source of inspiration and motivation.

A clear vision will help people decide to jump on board with you, as team members or clients. The purpose of the vision is to create your roadmap, to help you determine the steps you need to take to achieve your goals and the direction you move in for the business.

It will also help you to determine what clients you want to do business with and who you want to partner with. It is a great tool to give you clarity, direction and momentum. The great news is that creating a vision statement is even easier than setting your values.

To create your own vision statement, simply ask yourself this question (or get someone to ask you). If you were having a conversation with someone twelve months from now, everything you wanted to achieve for your business, you had, how would you describe your business? What would be happening? What are the results you would have achieved?

To make this an effective exercise you need to be as detailed as possible. I had a conversation with a business owner just last week and asked that very question.

"I would have more clients and be making more money" she replied.

"Great" I said, "so, one extra client and another $4100 a month and all your goals would be achieved?"

"Of course, not" was her answer.

Can you see where this is going? More clients or more money or more time is not a vision. Twenty five percent increase in nett profit and working twenty percent fewer hours is a vision though. Be as specific as you can be. Really take the time to see it, feel it and get in touch with what you want. Then you have a true vison statement that will drive you and your business for the next twelve months.

Finally, you need to share your values and your vision.

Here is a simple test I always use. If I pulled up outside your home in my car and invited you to get in, one of the first questions you would ask me would be "where are we going?" And yet, many of us invite our team (as per the extended definition from earlier) to get into the car that is our business on a daily basis without sharing where you we are going, why we are going there, what is at the destination and how we propose to reach it.

Does that sound familiar? As a business owner have you failed to share your vision and your driving values with your team. Have you worked for a business that failed to share that with you? It is really disheartening to see good people leaving what could be a great business because they were never given the opportunity to share in the dream of the owner.

Don't let that happen to you. Sharing your values and the vision you have for your business will help you to get the right people on board, as team members, partners and clients. Everyone wants to be part of a motivated, passionate team moving forward with purpose. if you don't take the opportunity to share the values, the vision, the dream then you run the risk of struggling to get the right people around you and the success you strive for becomes an unnecessarily uphill battle.

There is an old saying in business culture that a fish rots from the head down. If you want to drive your business to that true status, to give you more time, control and money then you have to make sure that your fish doesn't rot and that means driving a positive, value based culture. That way you can get great people to join you on the journey and make your business dreams a reality.

Don't let culture slip by you. Make it a priority by following these simple steps there is a lot more easy to use resources at www.haveabusinessnotajob.com to help you.

CHAPTER 8

Get More Done But Not By You

'Never automate something that should be eliminated and never delegate something that should be automated'

THE ART OF DELEGATION

One of the greatest skills you can master as a business owner is that of delegation. Once you understand the concept of focusing your efforts on what is the highest and best use of your time you will find that you are probably doing lots of things in your business that can easily be done by someone else. The hard part is letting go.

In this section I am going to show you some very simple rules which will empower you to become an extremely effective delegator. In turn, this will free your time like you have probably never imagined. The most successful people I work with are brilliant delegators. They truly understand the value of their time and delegate accordingly.

Delegation is a lot more than just passing a task on to someone else. It is a complete tool, which you can use to effectively run your business and make sure that you spend time working on it, not just in it.

When I first start coaching a client I ask them to do two things. The first is to list their frustrations and the second, as you have read, is to complete a SWOT analysis. (Remember there is one at the back of this book for you to use). Invariably, one of the frustrations, usually closer to the top of the list, is not enough time to work on the business.

Most small business owners (and a few big ones as well) spend too much time in the day to day operations of their business and there is simply not enough time left to work on business development. I have said on more than a few occasions throughout this book how important innovation is. You can't hope to be innovative while you are toiling away at the coal-face of your business.

Let's start changing that now and learn how to effectively delegate.

There are a couple of very simple rules of effective delegation the primary one is to remember that delegation is about asking someone else to take responsibility for something. It is not just about giving someone a task, that's just simple task management. If you really want to be a great delegator, you need to pass on the responsibility for whatever you are delegating. Letting go can be a struggle at first but believe me, once you get the hang of it, it will change your life. When I spoke about completing your one page business plan in this book, I mentioned that one of the targets may be to find more time for yourself. That can only come from effective delegation. I'll get to exactly how you do that shortly but first let's just finish off the rules.

"If you want to do a few small things right, do them yourself.

If you want to do great things and make a big impact, learn to delegate."

John C Maxwell

Once you understand that delegation is about passing on responsibility then you need to understand the rule of security. Simply put this is a way of making sure you can be secure in transferring that responsibility. To get there, you need simply ask yourself three questions:

1. Are the expectations associated with the delegation crystal clear?

2. Does the person you are delegating to have all of the skills tools and resources available to them to take on the responsibility?

3. Is there a very clear reporting process in place for them to report back to you?

If you can confidently answer 'yes' to all three questions, then the delegation should work. There are however a few ways in which all this great delegation planning can go wrong.

Firstly, when I say there needs to be a clear reporting process in place, I mean a process to report on progress and completion of the task. What happens if part of the way through the task, the person you have delegated to gets stuck and doesn't know what to do next? They will ask you. Beware this is the first way your house of delegation can come crumbling down around you.

Many years ago, when my son Nicholas was very young I wanted to become the best father I could be to him and his sister. So I took myself off to parenting classes. I completed courses in Positive Parenting, Toddler Taming but the most valuable course I ever did was the Parent Effectiveness Training. If you are reading this and have small children, stop and make a quick note to see if there is a Parent Effectiveness Training course available near you. It quite literally changed my life as a parent. Now, why am I sharing this with you? Because, that course taught me an invaluable tool which I have now used in every business I have coached. I have passed this tool on to more people than I could remember and I have never had anyone (ever!) not tell me how amazing it was. Like many truly amazing learnings, it is very simple but once you get it, it will help make you a master at delegation.

So, with the Problem Ownership tool you follow this very simple process:

1. When someone comes to you with a problem, ask yourself; "is there really a problem or are they just sharing?"

2. If there is a problem, next ask yourself "is this problem mine or theirs?"

3. If the problem is yours then you can go about solving it.

4. If the problem is theirs then your job is to coach them to find a solution for themselves.

The Problem Ownership Plan *

YOURS
- you have to solve it

NO PROBLEM

THEIRS
- you coach them to solve it

Most situations fit into one of the above three categories.
* credit to Thomas Gordon

BUSINESS

Ask coaching questions to become delegation royalty

Taking this back to delegation it means that once you have delegated the task, if that person comes back to you with a problem, follow the ownership process. If it is their problem then you have to coach them, not take the task back. That's a real delegation rookie error right there. Don't get caught! Until people get used to your new found delegation commitment they will try and give the responsibility back to you.

How do you resist their efforts to return the responsibility to you? Using some simple coaching terms will help immensely. Here are three simple questions you need to ask when your delegate returns to you with a problem:

1. What is your biggest challenge
2. What are some options
3. Who else can you ask for help?
4. Specifically, what do you want from me?

Master these four questions and you will become Delegation Royalty very quickly.

Now that you know how to delegate, the question is what can you delegate? This is the second way your delegation plans can fall into a heap, delegating the wrong things. Here is a very simple process.

1. Make a list of everything you do in your business, the task for which you are personally responsible.

2. Work through that list and ask yourself at each point, does this really need to be done. Strike out anything that you realize doesn't need to be done Remind yourself of this quote: "The most dangerous phrase in the language is, we've always done it this way." - Admiral Grace Hopper.

3. Take what's left and ask yourself, which of these tasks absolutely HAVE to be done by me.

4. Whatever is left can be delegated

Finally, If you want to work out who to bring into your business to perform those tasks, whether it be an employee, or as an outsource, try using my Mastermind Pit Crew Exercise.

Start in the centre of the sheet and write down all the things that are essential for you to do, either because you love doing it or because you are the most highly qualified. This is what I call your genius. Once you have that listed, use the outer circles to answer the question: 'For me to be in my genius, I need someone to……"

Now you know what to delegate, how to effectively delegate and a clear picture of who you need in your business in order to make that happen.

THE PIT CREW™

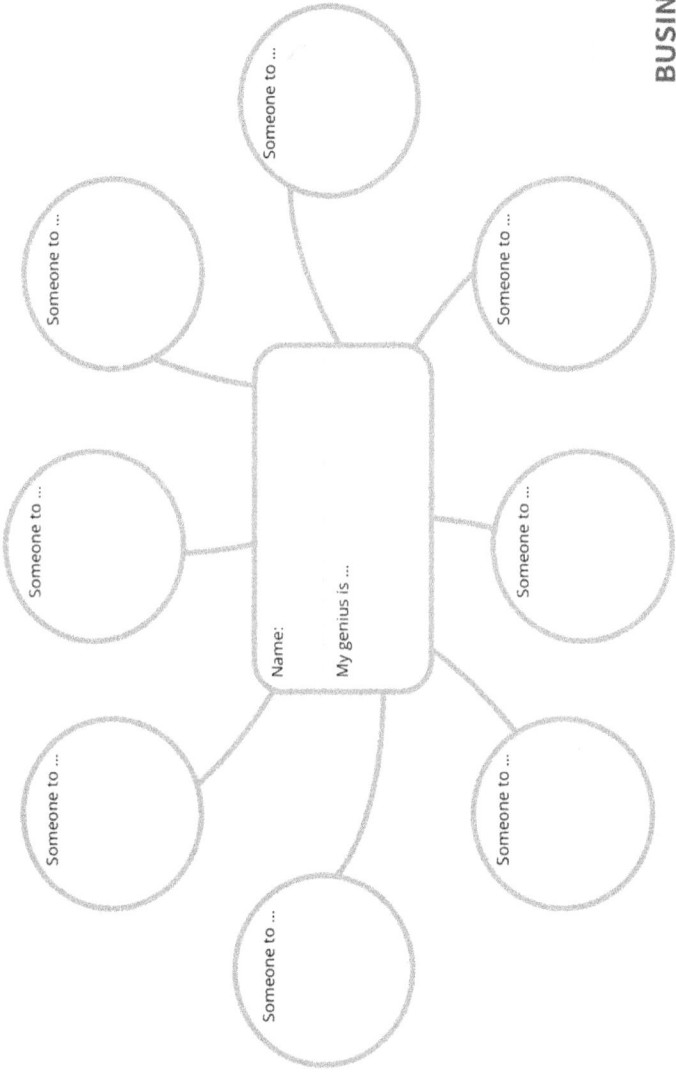

BUSINESS

Name:

My genius is ...

Someone to ...

Someone to ...

Someone to ...

Someone to ...

Someone to ...

Someone to ...

Someone to ...

Someone to ...

CHAPTER 9

Why Cash Flow Is Queen

You've probably heard the saying that cash is king. Well, if that is true then cash flow would be the queen. That's because understanding cash flow is vital to success in your business. And yet I've met many business owners who have little understanding of cash flow or accounting principles generally. Worse still I often come across business owners who say that they have no interest in learning and no desire to improve their knowledge in that regard. That's crazy talk!

If you don't understand what is happening with the finances in your business, you could very well be heading for disaster and it may be too late by the time you discover it. Understanding the accounting and financial management aspect of your business will allow you to stay ahead of any problems, to properly and effectively plan and to be able to take advantage of looming opportunities.

The great news is that it is getting easier than ever to grasp a basic understanding of financial principles. With development in online learning and, more importantly, development of accounting and reporting software, getting your head around the finances in your business can be very simple.

Understanding Cash Flow

If you are new to business take some time to learn about cash flow and financial management. Here are some simple ways to achieve the basics:

- Take an online course
- Check out YouTube
- Ask your accountant or bookkeeper to spend some time with you and teach you the basics
- Attend an adult learning course

Having a grasp of the basics will be enough to enable you to manage the financials in your business. You need to be able to read a profit and loss statement, understand the purpose of a balance sheet and understand the concept of cash flow. If that is all you get to master that will suffice. The rest, such as tax planning, deductibility, EBIT calculations and forecasting can be left to the experts and we will talk about that a little later in this chapter.

WHAT IS CASH FLOW?

Understanding the difference between cash flow and profit and loss will help you immensely. Profit and loss will tell you at the end of any accounting period - whether it be monthly, quarterly or yearly what your bottom line is. It will tell you how much money you brought into your business, how much you spent and how much you made or lost at the end of the period. Profit and loss is about exactly that, money and how much you made or lost.

Cash flow, on the other hand, is not so much about money but about time. Cash flow will tell you when money is due to come into your business and when it is due to go out and that is why it is imperative that you understand it.

Cash flow is one of the financial areas in of your business you can actually control and it is something that reports in advance. In other words, a cash flow forecast report will tell you what is about to happen, before it actually happens, whereas a profit and loss reports after the event when there is little or nothing you can do to change the nett outcome.

So, understanding cash flow and being able to read a cash flow forecast will drive your business planning and the day-to-day management of your business. Let me give you some very simple examples.

CASH FLOW FORECASTING

If you have a cash flow forecast for the next month and it shows that at the end of the month you will need to have spent more than you will make then you have the opportunity to take some corrective action. You may choose to delay some spending in the coming month, perhaps you could negotiate longer trading terms with a supplier or you may be able to bring money in faster. A word of caution, though, if you are looking to negotiate longer trading terms be careful to consider your cash flow position over the same longer period of time. Otherwise you may be solving a problem for this month but creating a bigger one in the next month.

When it comes to bringing money in faster there are also some simple things you can do. Look at your debtors and chase those that owe you money, calling them, or emailing and asking for payment of outstanding accounts can fast track money coming in. Don't be shy. If you've provided the goods or services, then you are entitled to be paid and someone else's cash flow issue doesn't and shouldn't be yours.

I often speak with small business owners who don't want to appear to be desperate for money, so they won't ask to be paid or to hurry debtors along. Saving face like that is fine but it won't help you when you need to pay your bills or to get your own team's wages paid. Like most things in business and like the vast majority of the secret I share with you in this book, there are some exceptions.

If you need to chase payments make sure you use some discretion. Look at those that owe you money. If it is a large customer and they always pay you then perhaps you can allow them more time or even a polite phone call. Don't damage a long-erm relationship for a short-term gain. I've always found that being honest with your debtors works, particularly if they are in a similar sized business to you. You will most likely find that they will understand your need to manage cash flow very well and will do what they can to accommodate your needs. If your debtors are large companies, don't be bullied. Set very clear expectations around getting paid and insist on compliance. They won't respect the value of your business if you don't.

So use discretion, follow up on payments which you believe you are entitled to but keep the balance between getting paid and maintaining good quality long-term relationships. Remember, though, that no matter how good a relationship may seem, if it all one sided then it is bad for your business.

My friend best-selling author Michael Yardney takes the view that his business isn't one which chases money. He is in the position of being able to take that stance, but it has come from many years developing a reputation in the marketplace and setting clear expectation around the value and cost of his services. Because of those clear expectations and the belief that Michael has in the value of what his business provides, he always gets paid.

CASH FLOW SHORTFALL SOLUTIONS

If you don't have debtors, you can follow up on and you can see a shortfall in your cash flow forecast then you may be able to get orders brought forward. I am never a fan of discounting as I discuss in this book, it only creates loyalty to the discount and not to the product or service but used strategically it can be a powerful tool. If you can see the cash shortage looming, look to offer your products or services at a discount for an early purchase and payment.

If you don't want to offer a discount (and I'm OK with that) then look to ask for business. Review your contacts and pipeline and see if there is anyone who has made an enquiry with you or has purchased goods or services from you in the past who you may be able to sell to now. You may want to offer a small value-add opportunity as an enticement.

"Making more money will not solve your problems if cash flow management is your problem"

Robert Kiyosaki

When my business was in its early days and I went through cash flow shortages I would simply review my database and contact potential clients. I would try to convert them to paying clients even if it was with a one-off product as opposed to my usual longer-term engagement. You may be surprised. I often found that potential clients had been meaning to contact me and my call to them was the catalyst they needed to proceed. More often than not they appreciated the contact. And if they weren't quite ready to buy from me, they still appreciated the reactivity.

A final word of caution, don't sound desperate. Have you ever been speaking with a salesperson who sounded desperate for the sale? It's off-putting isn't it? No matter how dire your cash flow position may appear to you, keep your game face on. Don't let on that you urgently need the money. It creates concerns around the quality of the goods or services you will offer and it may also give the bargain hunters a chance to talk you into a price, which in any other circumstances, you would never agree to.

The other step available to you is to negotiate with your creditors. Negotiating favourable terms at the start of the relationship is ideal. Be clear around their expectations and then work hard to meet them. If you have been dealing with a creditor for some time and you have always traded within the agreed terms it will make asking for some variation a lot easier. In most cases your creditors will be looking to maintain business with you and as long as you don't unfairly take advantage of the relationship then leeway will be forthcoming. Be careful, though, if you ask for extended terms, make sure you keep to your word. In this fast-paced digital world we live in, your integrity and your reputation are still paramount.

So, what if you can't follow up on debtors and you have exhausted all of the potential sales in your pipeline and you still don't have enough to cover the looming cash flow shortage? Well, this is where a good relationship with your bank becomes important.

GET FRIENDLY WITH YOUR BANK

Banks get a lot of bad media and often its rightly deserved. However, having a good relationship with your business bank will become an essential ingredient in your success formula. When I first started in business in 1990, I got to sit with the manager of my local bank branch and he was able to make decisions to approve funding for my business with a handshake.

Times have changed. Banks have centralised their business banking and decision-making is often not done by the person you initially work with. But getting to know your business banker and establishing a strong relationship with them is vital. It is also in this process that your clear understanding of your financial reporting will be essential. In any discussions you have with your bank, they will be looking to see that you truly understand the financial management aspect of your business.

One of the important tasks in building the relationship with your bank is to get them to understand your business. They need to know what you do, how you do it and what your business philosophy is. Having a banker who truly understands your business and your industry will make the process easier and more beneficial to both parties.

Remember, banks are in the business of lending money, so they actually want you to borrow. It is up to you to make sure that borrowing suits your planning and that it fits in with your financial forecasting. Working with major banks and financiers will mean that responsible lending practices will apply and that will protect you to some degree.

HOW DO YOU GET YOUR BANK TO KNOW YOU AND YOUR BUSINESS?

I had a business banker from a major bank call me once a few years ago and say she wanted to come and see me and look at how the bank can work with my business. Within a few minutes of arriving at my office she asked me what it was I did. She had obviously spent no time researching before the appointment, so the whole process was little more than a waste of my time. Here is what I learned from that experience:

- Ask your business banker to come and see you.

- Send then some information about you and your business.

- Tell them you would like to review your banking and see what they can do to help you grow your business.

- Let them know you are shopping around. The banking market is competitive.

- Send them a link to your website and ask them to have a look so that they have an understanding of your business.

- If your industry has some peculiarities around it, give them some information about that. Perhaps it is very seasonal or perhaps it is a new or emerging market and they need to be aware of the opportunities and challenges.

- Be clear about what you want from the bank. If you aren't sure of what you need most, get advice from your bookkeeper or accountant or ask another business owner. I often talk with my clients about the importance of having a group of other business owners around you to bounce ideas off, to learn from and share with.

GET FRIENDLY EARLY

Following these simple steps will help you on the way to establishing a healthy relationship with the bank. But here is another and probably the most crucial hint… Establish your relationship with your bank early. Get to know them and have them know you when you are in the early stages of your business.

If you are reading this and have been in business for some time and don't have a relationship with your bank, now is the time to take action. It is going to be much harder to try and establish a relationship if you first approach the bank when you are in a cash flow crisis. It will also be much easier to ask the bank for support if they already know you and your business well.

What if you haven't got that relationship and you are in need of support from your bank right now? Well, the good news is that you can still ask the bank for support, but you will need to do a little ground work first. Or you could consult with a good broker. Andrew Mirams from Intuitive Finance in Melbourne is a client of mine and a superb finance broker. Seeing what he can do with finance strategies for his clients has affirmed my view on the value of a good broker.

Again it will be important to help them to have a thorough understanding of your business and your industry, but armed with that information they should be able to hunt around with the banks and commercial financiers to find the best solution for your particular needs. A good business accountant will most certainly have access to a broker they can refer you to.

OK, so what if the situation arises where you have a good relationship with your bank, but they just aren't supporting you at a time when you most need it? I actually had that experience with a client recently.

Real-life client success story

I was working with a national company operating with a $25 million turnover that had been working with one bank for more than 15 years. The company hit some cash flow issues and could see there would be a substantial shortfall, which was likely to last them the next three months. They needed their bank to support them.

Ironically what they were asking for from the bank was no different to what they had in fact received from the bank in previous years. The differences were that their trading figures were not as strong and they had a new banking relationship manager. I had been coaching them for a short time but I was aware of the challenges in their business and their industry, so we were able to put an action plan in place.

The plan is the very same action plan I have used with clients before and one which you can use if you find yourself in the same position. Here is what we did:

- Instructed the accountants to prepare and certify cash flow forecasts and profit and loss forecast documents.

- Prepared a funding proposal.
- Called a meeting with the bank and insisted that decision-makers were present. We got some push back on this, but we persevered. By showing the bank that we were serious about finding a solution and that we wanted to have decision-makers involved gave them a clear signal that we knew what we were doing.
- Asked the accountants to be present for the meeting.

When we prepared the funding proposal, apart from the cash flow and profit and loss reports, we openly addressed the issues the business had faced, which led to the cash shortage and then clearly laid out the steps which were being taken to address each issue.

We time-lined each step and made sure we included processes to test and measure the effectiveness of each step. Once complete, the funding proposal read like a very clear story of how the business got to where it was, what it was doing to address it and exactly how the bank could support it. The end result was the approval of the facilities needed.

Now don't think for a moment that it only worked because of the size of the business. Over time I've coached businesses with as little as $500, 000 turnover and helped them through similar processes.

It is, of course, one of the advantages of having a business coach, someone who can be an "unreasonable friend" to keep you accountable but also someone who can provide that objective support and guidance when you need it most.

THE BOTTOM LINE ON BUDGETS

An integral part of any business planning and financial management is a budget. There is an old saying that a failure to plan is a plan to fail and I think the very same can be applied to budgeting.

I use budgeting in my business and with my clients in two ways. Firstly, to forecast expenditure and manage the timing of major cost centres and secondly as a goal-setting tool for income. The great news is that budgeting has really never been easier. There are a wide range of budgeting tools available online and as apps, or you can work with your accountant or bookkeeper to create budgets with you.

Whichever way you choose, make sure the budgets are both complete and realistic. By that I simply mean that you need to make sure you have all expenses accounted for. You will have fixed costs such as rent or lease expenses, wages, insurances, licensing and utilities and you will have variable expenses such as the cost of goods. Ensure you have them all covered and I prefer to err on the side of caution, which involves overestimating on costs and allowing for increases across the year. On the realistic front, keep in mind that costs will increase as your business grows so if you can foresee growth (and I certainly hope you can) then allow for that as well.

Like most planning, when I am budgeting, I like to start with the end in mind and work back from there. So, a simple budget can start with how much money you want to earn in the next year. By that I mean how much retained profit do you want to have accumulated by the year's end. Here, turnover is not the right ingredient to consider. That will come at the next stage of the calculation. Remember, you have a huge turnover, but if the margins on your product or service are small then you may not achieve retained profit goals. This is particularly so if your sales change or your variable costs vary significantly.

Once you are clear about that you can start to work backwards. In order to achieve your target income, you can determine the turnover you need after adding your desired retained profit to the total of your fixed and variable costs (allowing for variations and increases). From there you can determine your peak selling periods and then budget each month accordingly. Accounting programs such as Xero will then allow you to upload your budget and with dashboard reporting you should be able to maintain a monthly watch on your progress.

- In my business I receive a dashboard report each month which tells me the key financial drivers. I need to know:

- The value and age of my debtors.
- My actual performance as against my budget in terms of turnover.
- My actual retained profit.
- My cash at bank.
- My performance this year as against the same period last year and
- My actuals as against budget year to date.

With that information I am able to have a quick snapshot of the financial health of my business. If I notice anomalies in that report I can then look at the profit and loss and drill down further.

GET HELP

Finally, the one important step encourage all of my clients to do is to seek professional help for your budget requirements. When you are running your business there are huge demands on your time. The very best thing that you can do to foster proper management and active growth is to understand what is the highest and best use of your time and it is rarely "doing the books" and yet that is exactly what many small business operators do.

The logical process is usually fairly simple and is a matter of basic math. If the cost of a bookkeeper can be easily offset by the increased revenue you can generate by utilising your "doing the books" time then the logical decision is to outsource the bookkeeping. Even if you attend to your bookkeeping after hours, consider whether that time could be better spent with family or working either on you or on your business through planning or product or service development as opposed to working in it with your books.

So, the logical decision is a relatively easy one. The tough part I often find with clients I start working with is the psychological decision of "letting go". There is a certain amount of psychological comfort in knowing that you are in control of the business by attending to the bookkeeping yourself. If you find that you are afraid of letting go and think that you need to maintain control of the bookkeeping in order to maintain control of your business....you're wrong!

As my friend Michael Yardney often says, you wouldn't do your own dentistry or surgery, so if you're not a bookkeeper or accountant why would you do that for yourself?

This is a great example of mastering the science and art of delegation – a secret I shared with you elsewhere in this book. It's easier to do it myself is one of the great fallacies of business management. I went through this process in my own business a number of years ago.

Then, my wife Caroline, would attend to the books in our business and I had to coach her through the letting go process.

She is now an ardent fan and a great spokesperson for the benefits of retaining a professional bookkeeper. Letting go has allowed her to concentrate on delivering outstanding and innovative service to our clients and to focus on the inspirational and innovative ways we stay in contact with our clients. Caroline's "fear" of letting go quickly dissipated once she saw the benefits. Jac Gallagher from Notch Above has made a substantial difference to our business and the revenue we've created by allowing Caroline to focus on her strengths. This has paid Jac's fees many times over and not to mention the balance it has brought to Caroline's personal time.

LEARN HOW TO LET GO

If you are having trouble letting go of the bookwork in your business here are few hints to help you take that step:

- Choose a good bookkeeper. Ask your accountant for a recommendation. Alternatively talk to your network of other business owners (we have spoken before of the importance of maintaining even a small network of like-minded individuals in the same position as you for support and guidance) or ask your coach if you have one.

- Get a fixed price quote for the bookkeeping work. If a bookkeeper isn't prepared to give you a fixed price, find another one.

- Spend some time with them explaining what you want them to do and how you want to be reported to.

- With cloud-based software, most bookkeeping can be completed remotely so don't worry about finding extra space in your business premises. This may be particularly relevant if you operate a home office.

- Meet with them at regular intervals even if it is by phone or video. Monthly or quarterly is a good interval. If you need to stay in control at first, make it monthly and move to quarterly meetings as your confidence grows.

Your bookkeeper should be able to help you review your budgets and maintain cash flow forecasts. That way you will have control over the financial success of your business without having to spend hours "doing the books".

PAY YOURSELF FIRST – ALLOCATE A PERCENTAGE TO INVEST IN YOU.

The last aspect of the secret to success with financial management is something I share with all of my clients. At first it may seem a little strange but once implemented it will make a significant difference to the way you view your business. The last little secret is to pay yourself first. Yes, that's right, before you pay your bills, pay yourself. Now, obviously, that is working on the basis that you have a sound business and your forecasts are reasonably healthy. This is more of a psychological strategy than a financial one.

Let's be clear. I'm not for a minute advocating that you don't pay your creditors, that would be silly. What I am saying, however, is that if you get into the habit of paying yourself first, you will value your worth to the business. That, in turn, will help you stay motivated and so your business will grow.

It may sound simplistic, but it is a strategy I have used with countless businesses with great success. Once you know that your hard work and effort will be rewarded by being paid each week then you will have a clear head to focus on generating the revenue to pay your creditors. Trying to be motivated with an empty wallet is a challenge few can master. It's a bit like trying to think on an empty stomach or function without a coffee. Try it and watch your motivation increase and your business grow as a result.

Keeping a track of the finances in your business doesn't have to be as daunting as you think. Having a professional working with you will help as will having a basic understanding of financial reporting. Remember, you don't have to be an accountant, you can hire one of them.

Now that you have a better understanding about cash flow, let's move on to....

CHAPTER 10

Have Fans Not Clients

There are few more powerful strategies in business than a dedication to customer service. It is often talked about, regularly championed and frequently put forward by a business as their unique selling proposition (USP).

Sadly it is also most often the one business strategy which is well designed but poorly executed. Unfortunately, for some businesses, over promising and under delivering has become almost an art form.

HUMANS AREN'T GOING ANYWHERE

A few years ago there were dire predictions that the rise of online shopping would spell the end of any traditional bricks and mortar stores or offices. Recently I attended a conference where a futurist predicted that our current office buildings would become wastelands of the future. The one aspect which these predictions fail to take into account, however, is the need for human interaction.

There is no doubt that online shopping for products and services has made life more convenient but even online retailers are now moving to brick and mortar stores. A simple business proposition that "people buy people" still stands and I suggest will do so for a very long time to come.

In the retail space, shopping centres are on a resurgent path as developers realise that shopping on the internet does not afford retail shoppers the opportunity for interaction with other human beings. They have, quite cleverly, realised that shopping centres are in many ways the modern day community hubs that provide the local community with a place to gather.

SERVICE STILL MATTERS

Let's not imagine that this philosophy applies only to the retail market, however. Clever use of technology can make doing business with you more convenient, but it will not replace the need for you to deliver personal service at some stage in the transaction.

No doubt there are thousands of people working in Silicon Valley right now developing ways to automate what we do on a daily basis as well as ways to automate whatever business you are currently in or are planning to enter. That very development will, of itself, create business opportunities we have not even thought of yet. But it will not replace humans (not for a while anyway!)

My doctor has an online booking system where I can log on, choose an appointment time that best suits me and make the appointment. I then receive a text to confirm the appointment and even a reminder text an hour or so before the appointment. When I arrive at the surgery, I can let the doctor know I have arrived by registering on the iPad in the waiting room and I can even place an order for a tea or coffee while I am at it. But… when my turn comes to see the doctor, I see a human being. And

it is at that point where his ability to provide me with the service
I want will determine whether I remain as a patient.

Let's look, then, at what makes great service, how we can
deliver it and importantly how we can maintain it. As true as it
is that technology will not replace service, there is little doubt
that it can enhance great service and enable your business to
deliver it consistently. Tony Allesandra once said, "Being on par
in terms of price and quality only gets you into the game.
Service wins the game".

Great service is easy to promise but worthless if the promise
is not delivered on and worse than worthless if it is delivered but
inconsistently. Imagine going to your favourite restaurant
wondering if the food was going to be any good each time? The
fact is you wouldn't return there.

WHAT DO YOUR CLIENTS THINK ABOUT YOU?

Now is a great time to start to ask yourself if your clients
wonder that each time they deal with your business.

Here are five simple steps you can implement in your
business to ensure you are delivering service standards which
will place you well ahead of your competition.

1. Make it easy to do business with you.

Again, these principles apply no matter what your business is, what service or product you deliver, or even how you deliver it. One of the very fundamentals of customer service is to make it so that your customers find it not only easy but also a pleasure to do business with you.

Have you ever tried to buy something but found the process was just too complex, too many questions or not enough understanding of your needs so in the end you gave up and went somewhere else? Or have you ever been a repeat customer of a business yet every time you return, they ask you the same questions or treat you like you have never done business with them before? So, how do you make it easy to do business with you?

2. Make it very clear who you are and what you do.

Having a cryptic business name may seem like a very cool and chic idea sitting around a dinner table over a glass of wine but if the name of your business is too cryptic then you are just creating an unnecessary hurdle. I once met a marketing consultant who named his business using Latin terms. The reality is that lawyers and Catholic priests are probably the last two sets of students of Latin today, a narrow market indeed.

Names can therefore be too clever and too cryptic. It doesn't mean you can't use some flare or even have a name which begs the question, "What is that?" but anything that is simply out of left field will confuse your potential customers or make it far too difficult to find you, let alone do business with you.

3. Be visible.

If you have a retail shop, make sure it is easy to find. Clear signage, easy access and parking will make coming to your store a simple process rather than a chore.

4. Update details

There are few more frustrating things than looking a business up on the internet only to find that their contact details are wrong. Make sure you are regularly updating records. If your number or email changes then make sure your website is updated. Oh, and please, don't use a generic web domain for your email address. Spend the time and money (it is not a big investment) to have an email which matches your domain name and therefore the name of your business. Sales@alisonscakes.com.au sounds so much more professional and will be easier to remember and contact than alisonscakes@gmail.com. Simply put, make sure your customers can find you.

5. Be very clear about the services you offer.

I have walked into retail outlets and have been totally confused about what the products or services on offer were. Sometimes it is because the place is a mess with no order or structure, sometimes it is because a business is trying to offer too much or too broad an offering and sometimes it is because the owner has wanted to project a certain image which is completely incongruous within the product and service being offered.

"MIKE" THE BIKE SHOP OWNER

I walked into a bicycle shop once. While there were a few bikes on display, the owner was a motor racing fanatic and had decorated the entire business with motor racing memorabilia. The message was confused and it didn't give me a very clear and strong message that this business was all about bikes. It wasn't easy to do business there because I didn't know if they wanted to sell me motor racing signs or a bicycle. I loved the owner's passion for something but that needed to be at home, in his study or the pool room.

6. Complete the transaction

Once it is clear who you are, where you are and what you sell, the next step is to make it simple to complete the transaction.

"TRUDY" THE CAFE OWNER

I recently went to a café for breakfast. It came highly recommended by friends and I had been looking forward to a leisurely Sunday breakfast. The food was above average and so was the service, however when I came to pay, they did not accept credit card and also placed a five per cent surcharge on debit cards. Cash, they said was their preferred option. For me, they made it too difficult to complete the transaction.

Why would I pay a surcharge on my debit card when the café not more than two blocks away provided food and service of equivalent quality and is happy to accept any of my cards with no additional fees? It is short-term thinking and presenting a potential barrier to doing business. I don't know why a business owner would do it.

If you want to absorb your bank fees, then either negotiate a better deal with your bank (we talked about that in the chapter on cash-flow or absorb it into your charges). I would rather pay a little extra on the menu than be presented with a surcharge at the end. I know I am not alone there. It is not just about payment, though, make sure it is easy to complete the transaction beyond payment as well.

If you are selling large items or online, ensure delivery is not a challenge for your customer. If you are offering a service as opposed to a product, make sure that you can deliver the service in a manner and timeframe which best suits the customer.

GREAT SERVICE IS A CULTURE

Great service can be as simple as thanking existing customers. Believe me that would be a great start and once you have that in place then you can propel the concept from there. The next simple step is to think of ways to make it a pleasure to do business with you. Great service is a culture. It starts at the very top of every business and is the responsibility of every person within the business.

- Thank them
- Deliver over and above
- Remember it is the one percenters that make the difference
- Make them feel special
- Break the rules... don't do things the way everybody else does.

The very best marketing strategy, the best branding, design and even the greatest website or business premises are of no value if the service delivery is poor. So how do you deliver great service? Here are some steps that you can take and apply right now in your business.

1. Think critically about what your client is looking for.

This relates to the identification of the true product (you read a whole lot more about that in the chapter on product in this book). Once you have a true understanding of the emotion behind the purchase that your clients are making then developing a compelling service model will be relatively easy.

2. Look at the very best competition you have.

Experience the service they deliver. It's easy to beat it once you understand it and have true insight into what you are actually competing with.

"Customer service shouldn't just be a department, it should be the entire company"

Tony Hsieh

CHAPTER 11

The Power Of Partnerships

We've now moved into the final section, where I'll outline ideas on how you can build the right partnerships for your business.

In this chapter specially I am going to share with you the strategies I work on with my clients to help them accelerate growth without spending large amounts of money on marketing. This is not a social media marketing discussion; I will leave that to the social media experts. Here I am talking about good old-fashioned relationships and how, when worked with properly. they can add massively to your bottom line.

I am going to introduce you to range of partnership concepts and how each can contribute to your business (of course we will also talk about how to use social media and the internet to achieve many of these objectives). So, here is a quick look at the various partnerships we will discuss:

- Referral partners
- Alliance partners
- Endorsement partners
- Value add partners
- Financial partners.

It is a big list to get through so let's get started!

REFERRAL PARTNERS

Referrals are the most unbelievably cost-effective way of developing a business. While your competitors spend enormous amounts of money on hit or miss advertising campaigns, you can be engaging in phenomenal growth by simply asking existing clients, alliances, associates, friends, etc, to refer business to you.

One of the most interesting experiences I had in the development of my own business was that clients were continually telling me that they were very happy with the services that I provided, that I had helped them grow their businesses and that they found my assistance invaluable, but yet they were not referring clients to me.

I struggled with that because, although I knew my clients were telling me the truth, I was puzzled about why they weren't actually taking the next step and spreading that truth. The answer, in fact, turned out to be quite straightforward and that is that I simply hadn't asked them to.

So, one of the golden rules in developing a "knockout" referral system is to specifically ask your clients, friends, associates or alliances to actually refer business to you. You will find that once you ask for those referrals then they will quite readily and freely come to you.

There are some other important rules to be considered when developing a successful referral system. You must keep in mind that if someone is prepared to refer their client or contact to you then have regard to the fact that it's not only your reputation that comes into the mix but it is also their reputation as well. Personally, I am very careful about the referrals that I make. If I refer a client or an associate of mine to someone else, I only do so safe in the knowledge that the service or product that someone is providing, is in fact everything that they promise and that I have assessed it to be. It's important to recognise that asking someone to refer business to you is not just a casual exchange of information but that it's also a situation that requires a huge amount of trust and that in itself requires a great deal of respect.

Another important rule to remember is to offer an incentive for your referrals and to make sure that there is a clearly defined reward system in place. Take into consideration that rewards don't always have to be monetary or percentage based. Your reward or incentive could actually be as simple as saying "thank you".

At one of my recent seminars, I was discussing referrals with one of the attendees and he told me that he had a great referral system and that it was largely responsible for the growth of his businesses. He went on to say that he always made sure to thank a client who was referred to him for coming on board. I then asked him if he remembered to thank the person who had actually referred the new client and it turned out that he hadn't in fact been doing so. I spoke to him a few days later and he told me that after he had conducted an assessment of his referees, he discovered that although they were prepared to refer once they hardly ever referred a second time. The lesson to learn from all this, is that you must remember to thank the referring party. This let's them know that you appreciate the fact that they have extended their position of trust within their own network in referring business to you.

One of my own clients, who upon receiving a referral, automatically arranges to send out to the referrer a small gift basket. It doesn't cost her a lot of money, it's hand delivered so that it has a very personal touch and it shows her genuine appreciation.

When considering referrals in terms of a cost benefit analysis, remember that it is far more cost-effective than a hit or miss advertising campaign, which could in fact probably cost you substantially more than any reward which you may offer to people who refer business to you. The other aspect to keep in mind is that it may be worthwhile to offer incentives for referrals to your current clients. So, for example, you might say to a client or customer if you refer someone to me then you'll get a discount off your next purchase or you'll get a free a gift or something else that creates a genuine incentive for them to refer business across to you. Don't forget that referrals can also be a two-way street and this takes us to our next topic of discussion.

LEAD GENERATION

One of the greatest ways to secure referral business (second only to asking existing clients and customers to refer) is to develop great strategic alliances. This is a matter of looking at who else within either your industry or associated industries would be prepared to create an alliance with you in the interest of cross referrals and promotions. Let's look at the example of a web developer.

An example of a great strategic alliance that a web development company could strike would be with an internet service provider. Therefore, if I sign up with a provider, under the terms of the alliance, I am automatically referred to the web developer and vice versa. It's also very important to think outside the square when it comes to strategic alliances.

I have a client who runs a very successful national portraiture photography business who has developed alliances with what at first you may consider to be the most unlikely parties. For example, one of the most successful alliances that they created has been with a dental surgery! It seems quite a random pairing at first but consider that when a customer is waiting in the surgery for their appointment, they notice a lovely portrait on the wall and then after their dental work has been completed, the staff at the surgery offer them a gift certificate that entitles them to a special offer available through the photographic studio.

This is a perfect example of "thinking outside the square" when establishing strategic alliances, but you also need to make sure that this match occurs not only from an industry perspective but also from a business ethics and operations perspective as well. The last thing that you want to do, is to spend a lot of time developing a reputation for having an ethical business that has phenomenal customer service, only to strike a strategic alliance with a business who doesn't share those same qualities. This could then, in fact, make the alliance completely counter-productive.

Think creatively about potential alliance partners. It is well worth remembering that you are really looking for businesses which do business with your ideal client. Once you establish that as a guide then the limiting thoughts which often keep business owners thinking inside the square will quickly disappear. Think about your ideal client, what else do they spend money on? What are the other products and services they are likely to buy? It doesn't have to be linked to your business or even in the same product or service genre.

MARY AND PAUL THE COFFEE SHOP OWNERS

Mary and Paul run a small coffee shop in an inner Sydney suburb. Business is good but not growing and they are constantly facing new competition. Mary and Paul needed to have a look at how they can generate more business. The first thing they did was to conduct some research on their current customers, such as, who comes into their shop and what is the general demographic of an average customer. What they discovered was that early mornings were commuters, on their way to work. They were mostly in a hurry, bought take-away coffee and maybe a snack to go. On weekends those customers were replaced with cyclists looking for a break from cycling. After the early morning during the week came the mums (and a few dads) after dropping children at school. These customers were looking for a break, a relax and often a chance to meet and talk for a while. They were less hurried and so were likely to spend more time and therefore more money. The rest of the day was taken up with a mix of passing traffic, a few taxi and courier drivers and then parents in the afternoon after the school pick up, looking for a coffee and maybe a quick snack for the children. Now that they had this data, Mary and Paul can start to develop an alliance target list. (which is exactly what you should do in your business).

So what did Mary and Paul decide to do? They decided to target the local schools and kindergartens with an offer of value add such as a half-price cake with every coffee purchased for parents. But they went one step further. They also offered a program to each of those schools whereby any parent who shopped at their coffee shop would earn loyalty points for the school which would convert to a donation to the school fund on a quarterly basis.

It may not have been a lot of money, but it was clearly an added incentive for the parents to buy their coffee there. If Paul and Mary maintain great service and excellent quality products, then the choice becomes easy for those parents who then have the ability to enjoy a coffee and help the school at the same time. Once that alliance was in place, the school was happy to provide information to parents informing them of the alliance and encouraging them to coffee at Paul and Mary's.

Next they approached the local bike retailer and struck a similar deal. Here, though, it was as simple as saying that if the bike shop was prepared to refer its clients, then Mary and Paul would offer free coffee to the bike shop owner and staff. It was a small investment for a good return. It didn't stop there, because in addition they offered the bike shop the opportunity to place promotional material in the coffee shop, to give away a free bike service as a part of a coffee promotion. They also arranged to run a couple of bike information sessions on a Saturday morning at the coffee shop which generated interest for both businesses.

Paul and Mary also arranged with their local council to install some bike racks outside their shop and installed a water cooler, inviting cyclists to fill up their water bottles at no cost. Finally, they added some high energy and low-carb products to their range, aimed specifically at the cycling market and even named them using cycling terms.

For the couriers and taxi drivers, Paul and Mary contacted the taxi and courier companies (as well as speaking directly with the drivers) and advised they had introduced an SMS ordering service so that the drivers could order their coffee and it would be ready for them when they arrived. Adding a simple online payment arrangement made that an unbeatable program and it certainly generated a lot of business.

By now you can see that the opportunities are limitless. You have to start with an assessment of the clients you currently deal with, break those into segments and then think about what else those segments would buy. Once you have that done you can create an alliance target list and away you go.

Remember, creating an alliance is about creating mutuality however it does not have to always be an equal arrangement. If a business earns credibility and gratitude from its clients by referring to you, that is valuable in itself even if you are not able to refer as much business back to them. The other secret is to not be shy! Go ahead and ask for an alliance. If the other business owner isn't interested, move on and find someone who thinks like you.

Mary and Paul did exactly that. They had a few knockbacks in their quest to grow their business through alliances but once they had the system running, they added business year on year.

In fact, their first year of having all of those alliances in place saw an increase in profit of over 20 per cent. And the best part is it cost them very little other than time and some creative thinking.

ENDORSEMENT PARTNERS

What is an endorsement partner I hear you ask. Well, it is a very simple concept borrowed from the world of product advertising. How many times have you seen your favourite sports person or entertainer in an advertisement espousing the benefits of a product, encouraging you to buy it, or simply being seen in it, on it or using it?

The power of endorsement is phenomenal and the good news is that it is not limited to big business. You may not be able to afford to pay Roger Federer to endorse your product but there are certainly ways in which you can have your business endorsed - and often for little or no cost.

A very simple but effective endorsement partner process is to simply ask people who do business with you to endorse you. In terms of social media that may be asking people to like your Facebook page, to re-tweet your tweets or like or endorse what you are doing on Instagram. Asking clients to check in to Facebook when they are at your business premises, or doing business with you, will act as an active endorsement of your business without you having to spend a cent.

There are also plenty of sites which allow your clients to review the service and product you provide. Asking clients to review you on sites such as Trip Advisor is another great way of creating exposure and therefore marketing without you having to spend any money and without you having to provide the infrastructure to do so.

Of course, as with any exposure there is always a risk. Endorsements on these sites and social media platforms can be incredibly powerful but they can be equally damaging if they contain negative feedback about your business. This is by no means a set and forget strategy. You have to monitor what is being said about your business and be ready to address negative comments quickly. The good news is that if you maintain a focus on outstanding customer service then the likelihood that negative endorsements will be a significant issue is greatly diminished (there are unfortunately still some people who simply cannot be satisfied and there are also some trolls out there who will seek to ruin a reputation just for the fun of it).

The even better news is that for a relatively small investment you can have someone monitor everything that is said on the net and social media about your business so that you can respond quickly.

It is worth remembering that it is not just clients and customers who you can ask to endorse you. Think about the other businesses you do business with. Other businesses that you supply your products or services to may not be in a position to actively refer business to you but that does not preclude them from endorsing you.

"GERARD" THE GARDENER

Let's say you operate a commercial garden maintenance business. It may be that your commercial clients cannot directly ask people to come and do business with you, however, they may be prepared to endorse you by placing a sign on their premises or in their gardens or even something on their website to say that you look after their garden for them. Other business owners driving past may notice the quality of their garden, see the sign and contact you. They are not actively referring to you, but they are most certainly endorsing you.

These sorts of endorsements are not likely to create massive growth in your business, however, growth is really achieved in an incremental way where there are a range of strategies all delivering small increments of growth and cumulatively creating substantial growth for your business.

VALUE ADD AND FINANCE PARTNERS

The last two partnerships I am going to share with you are so closely linked I am going to deal with them together.

A value-add partner is simply another business which can add value to the product or service you provide. Value add partners may generate business for you via a cross referral program. You refer your clients to them for a value add service and they refer theirs to you or it may be that they pay you a fee (either a flat fee or a percentage of sale price) for every client you refer (a financial partner).

Let's have a look at some value-add partners first.

BEN THE REAL ESTATE AGENT

I was working with a real estate agent who was looking for ways to maintain relationships with his clients. Ben had a great relationship with sellers and buyers alike however once the property transaction was completed, his connection with both dropped off dramatically. He wanted a relationship- based business, but the people he was dealing with mostly saw it as transactional.

So, Ben started to look at what other products or services he could offer his client that would allow him to have contact with them after the property transaction had completed. Ben realised that people who buy and sell property also needed services such as insurance, finance and financial planning. This gave him the opportunity to create value add and financial alliances. Here is how he did it.

Firstly, Ben contacted a quality finance broker he had worked with in the past. He made sure the broker was qualified and accredited and had a similar commitment to excellent service as he did. He then proposed that he would refer his buyers to the broker and that for every buyer who retained the broker to assist with their purchase, Ben would receive a flat fee from the broker.

This was actually a multi-layered alliance which served a number of purposes. Firstly, it meant that Ben could stay involved with the buyer and help them to get the finance they needed to complete the transaction. That helped the property to settle, which in turn helped make the vendor happy (Ben's client) and so guaranteed his commission.

Secondly, it gave the buyers confidence and made them feel they were being well-looked after and cared for. Thirdly, it gave the broker good reason to refer any of his finance clients who were looking to sell their property to Ben. Finally, it earned Ben enough additional income to pay for his annual family holiday. It is what we would call a win-win-win situation!

Interestingly, though, it gets better still. When the finance broker conducted annual finance reviews of his clients he recommended they obtain a market appraisal of their property and if they were in Ben's area then you don't need to guess too hard which agent the broker would refer them to!

Next Ben did the same thing with an insurance agent and a financial planner. In each case he did not receive a fee back from the agent or the planner, so these were not financial alliances, but it did give Ben an opportunity to provide a value-add service to his buyers. That, in turn, furthered the relationship he had with the buyers. While he may not have received a financial benefit directly from the planner or the agent, he did have the opportunity to have them endorse his services (remember what we said about endorsement partners) and to market his services to their database over time.

Ben was also invited to attend and present at client information sessions for both partners, increasing his visibility and adding to his credibility as an expert in his industry.

While he was out striking up alliances for his real estate business Ben also decided to look at some creative "out of the box" ideas. This is an important part of alliance creation and I am always talking to my clients about the importance of thinking creatively. Ben always had a number of properties open for inspection on a Saturday, so he struck an agreement with the newsagent a few doors away from his agency.

Each Saturday morning for a month Ben would get to the newsagent early and stand at the front counter paying for the first 100 newspapers sold. It cost him a couple of hundred dollars but each week he had a chance to hand the customer a list of properties open for inspection that day. The newsagent was happy as it was guaranteed sales and was something a little different.

In return Ben promoted the newsagent on his website and of course promoted and endorsed the newsagency on social media.

One final little twist on this is that Ben had also struck a deal with the local coffee shop to provide the first 50 newspaper customers with a free coffee, which Ben paid a reduced price for. The whole exercise cost Ben a few hundred dollars but can you imagine what it did for his profile as a local trusted real estate agent?

FINDING A PARTNER

Finding a partner who can add value to the products and services you offer can benefit your business directly through referral fees and referred business and indirectly through cementing the relationship with your clients. There is an old saying that clients don't care how much we know until they know how much we care. Providing access to a value add partner may not immediately or directly add to the revenue stream in your business but it will most certainly add positively to the relationship you have with your clients and there is no doubt that will ultimately add to your revenue stream.

Let's recap on some quick partner strategies you can implement into your business straight away:

1. Develop a simple referral system.

Remember to thank both the referring party and the referred. Also, remember to make it simple and easy to follow.

2. Conduct research on your clients.

Who else would they do business with? If they do then others like them probably will as well. Once you are armed with that information approach those other businesses and establish a way to refer business between you.

3. Ask to be endorsed.

Not just from your clients but from anyone you deal with. Encourage social media endorsement but remember it is not a set and forget strategy.

Of course, this won't replace marketing or social media presence however I always encourage my clients to think of developing sales growth using a concentric circles model. It is far easier to sell your product to

- Someone who has already bought it
- Someone who knows someone who has bought it
- Someone who has had your product recommended to them (social proof)

Chasing new clients is essential but I think if there is an easy and a hard way, let's focus on the easy way.

Here is a copy of the SWOT Analysis Exercise that I mentioned earlier in the book:

SWOT Analysis- By Mark Creedon

SWOT analysis is a strategic planning method used to evaluate the Strengths, Weaknesses, Opportunities, and Threats involved in a project or in a business venture. It involves specifying the objective of the business venture or project and identifying the internal and external factors that are favourable and unfavourable to achieve that objective.

Strengths and Weaknesses	the **internal** environment - the situation **inside** the company or organisation	(i.e. factors relating to products, pricing, costs, profitability, performance, quality, people, skills, adaptability, brands, services, reputation, processes, infrastructure, etc.)	factors tend to be in the **present**
Opportunities and Threats	the **external** environment - the situation **outside** the company or organisation	for example, factors relating to markets, sectors, audience, fashion, seasonality, trends, competition, economics, politics, society, culture, technology, environmental, media, law, etc.	factors tend to be in the **future**

Swot Matrix

The SWOT analysis in this format acts as a quick decision-making tool, quite aside from the more detailed data that would typically be fed into business planning process for each of the SWOT factors. Here the 2x2 matrix model automatically suggests actions for issues arising from the SWOT analysis, according to four different categories:

	Strengths (Internal)	Weaknesses (Internal)
Opportunities (External)	**Strengths/Opportunities** **Obvious Natural Priorities** Likely to produce greatest ROI (Return On Investment). Likely to be quickest and easiest to implement. Probably justifying immediate action-planning or feasibility study. Executive question: "If we are not already looking at these areas and prioritising them, then why not?"	**Weaknesses/Opportunities** **Potentially Attractive Options** Likely to produce good returns if capability and implementation are viable. Potentially more exciting and stimulating and rewarding than S/O due to change, challenge, surprise tactics, and benefits from addressing and achieving improvements. Executive questions: "What's actually stopping us doing these things, provided they truly fit strategically and are realistic and substantial?"
Threats (External)	**Strengths/Threats** **Easy To Defend And Counter** Only basic awareness, planning, & implementation required to meet these challenges. Investment in these issues is generally safe and necessary. Executive question: "Are we properly informed and organised to deal with these issues, and are we certain there are no hidden surprises?" - and - "Since we are strong here, can any of these threats be turned into opportunities?"	**Weaknesses/Threats** **Potentially High Risk** Assessment of risk crucial. Where risk is low then we must ignore these issues and not be distracted by them. Where risk is high we must assess capability gaps and plan to defend/avert in very specific controlled ways. Executive question: "Have we accurately assessed the risks of these issues, and where the risks are high do we have specific controlled reliable plans to avoid/avert/defend?"

Exercise

List each of your businesses strengths, weaknesses, opportunities or threats in the table below and then outline how you plan to address each of the weaknesses/threats.

Strengths

Weaknesses

Opportunities

Threats

Bringing It All Together

This book has now given you the basic steps you need to take in order to build a business rather than just having a job. Many entrepreneurs start a business to give themselves more time, more money and more control, only to find themselves enslaved to the very thing they thought would give them freedom.

I don't want that for you. I want you to follow the processes I have set out in this book so that you can drive your business to where you want it to be. I want you to be able to step out of the business for weeks if not months at a time, safe in the knowledge that it will run itself nicely without you and that there will be just as much money in the bank when you come back as when you left.

Get time working for you at its highest possible state. Surround yourself with the right people, doing the right things, at the right time. Make sure you truly understand your product and focus on the transformation it brings to your clients and to your team. Engage with your clients where they are, at their level and in their emotional state and understand exactly what they want you to do for them.

Get clarity on your values, what drives you and what you truly want your business to achieve, to look and feel like.

Get these steps right and you will be well on your way to a level three business. You will have built a true business, not just a job all without nearly killing yourself in the process.

Where do you go from here?

The reality is that there is simply not enough room in this book for me to share all of the secrets I use with our Business Accelerator Mastermind clients.

I can however promise you this, take these lessons and apply them. Create new structure and habits in your business and you will undoubtedly reap the rewards.

There is no better time to start your journey to business success than right now. Take decisive action. Learn from my story and my experience and step boldly forward toward scaling your business up so you can scale out.

When you are ready to surround yourself with other successful business owners and truly scale your business, to earn twice as much money and spend half as much time in your business then go to -

www.metropolemastermind.com.au

Conclusion

Firstly, I want to congratulate you for reading all of this book. Most business owners and entrepreneurs say they want to improve themselves, but most are not prepared to do whatever it takes.

You, however, are different. You are one of the very few who are prepared to take the necessary steps, to do the hard yards and to dive deep into your business to make it the success that you deserve it to be.

Many years ago when I was in the depths of my burn out, when I wished that I had someone to give me the hand up I needed, the support I craved and the encouragement I deserved, I wish I could have read a book like this.

You do. The real power lies however not in reading the book but in taking action with what you have read. The important thing is not to go out and try and change everything all at once.

Everything we do in our Mastermind program is based on the concept of in time learning as opposed to in case. In other words, you look for the help you need right now and apply it so that you can get an immediate practical benefit, rather than trying to carry a whole bunch of 'stuff' in case you might need it at some stage.

Finally, trust yourself. Move forward with your business. The world needs more committed and passionate entrepreneurs just like you.

When you are ready for more support, greater accountability and invaluable group wisdom, head over to **www.metropolemastermind.com.au**. I'd love to chat with you about how we can get you to your goals faster

I wanted to finish this book with a quote from Caroline's Nuna Carrie Vella who at 90 shared this with me,

"Life is mostly froth and bubble, two things stand like stone. Kindness in another's trouble, Courage in your own."

Adam Lindsay Gordon

ABOUT THE AUTHOR

Mark Creedon has been helping business owners have the business and life of their dreams for over 15 years. He has guided, coached and motivated business owners to push their business to the next level, guiding them 'to grow beyond to go beyond'. After experiencing his fair share of painful trial and errors on his own path to success he has been able to refine his process into a bullet-proof system which helps entrepreneurs and business owners build a level 3 business of their own that works independently of them.

www.metropolemastermind.com.au

www.ingramcontent.com/pod-product-compliance
Lightning Source LLC
Chambersburg PA
CBHW070359200326
41518CB00011B/1993